Becoming Family

Becoming Family

HOW TO BUILD A STEPFAMILY THAT REALLY WORKS

Robert H. Lauer, Ph.D.
Jeanette C. Lauer, Ph.D.

Augsburg
MINNEAPOLIS

BECOMING FAMILY
How to Build a Stepfamily That Really Works

Scripture quotations are from the New Revised Standard Version Bible, copyright © 1989 by the Division of the Christian Education of the National Council of the Churches of Christ in the U.S.A. Used by permission.

Cover design by David Meyer. Book design by Michelle L. Norstad.

Library of Congress Cataloging-in-Publication Data
Lauer, Robert H.
    Becoming Family : how to build a stepfamily that really works / by
Robert H. Lauer and Jeanette C. Lauer.
    p. cm.
    Includes bibliographical references.
    ISBN 0-8066-3730-7 (alk. paper)
    1. Stepfamilies—United States—Psychology. 2. Stepparents—
United States—Attitudes. 3. Stepchildren—United States—
Attitudes. I. Lauer, Jeanette C. II. Title.
HQ759.92.L386 1999
306.874—dc21   98-48892
                                              CIP

The paper used in this publication meets the minimum requirements of American National Standard for Information Sciences—Permanence of Paper for Printed Library Materials, ANSI Z329.48-1984.   ∞ ™

Manufactured in the U.S.A.   AF 9-3730
03   02   01   00   2   3   4   5   6   7   8   9   10

To stepfamilies everywhere,
and to the loving family that nourishes us:
Jon, Kathy, Julie, Jeffrey, Kate, Jeff, Krista,
Benjamin, David, and John Robert

Contents

Preface

Demographers estimate that the stepfamily will be the main type of family in the United States by the year 2010. As of this writing, more than one of five families with two parents in the home is a stepfamily. Between seven and eight million children under age eighteen now live in a stepfamily. Therefore, if you are in a stepfamily, you share an experience with millions of other Americans.

You also face a common threat. The stepfamily is more fragile than other kinds of families. The rate of divorce is higher for stepfamilies than it is for first marriages or for second marriages where no children are involved. Building a lasting and rich family life is a crucial test of the power of grace and faith.

Despite the number of stepfamilies and the difficulties of maintaining a stable stepfamily, there is little in the way of Christian guidance and support for the special needs of stepfamilies. This book is an effort to fill the gap and to provide a practical, Christian guide for meeting the major challenges of stepfamily life. These challenges have been identified by professionals in the field of marriage and the family. We explain each of these challenges, show how they threaten the stability of the stepfamily and, if dealt with effectively, how they can enhance the solidarity of the stepfamily. We also demonstrate how these challenges can be met within the contexts of biblical teachings and actual experiences of Christian stepfamilies.

One of the steps we urge you to consider is to form or join a stepfamily support group. We believe that you can use this book as a basis for your discussions in such settings. To assist you, we have included an appendix with suggested activities and questions for small groups.

We would like to express our appreciation to all those stepfamilies who shared experiences with us and who encouraged us to pursue this book. They have helped us to understand both the struggles and the joys of stepfamily life.

"We're Going to Get It Right This Time"

"Joy"—that's how Marcia described the experience of telling her three children about her forthcoming remarriage. When Marcia and her husband divorced four years earlier, she had felt keenly "the loss of a family that we had all cherished." She was convinced that she was doomed to struggle through the foreseeable future as a single parent; she could not imagine getting married again.

Then "a very special man" unexpectedly came into her life. Bill was, as she put it:

> "A man with open arms, mind, heart, and soul. He had been married before but had no children. We hit it off from the first, and before long we began talking about marriage. Many of our discussions centered on my kids who were ten, twelve, and fourteen at the time. Bill was really looking forward to having a ready-made family, and we knew the kids were enthusiastic about Bill. But still we wrestled with the question of how to tell my children. It was crucial to both of us that they be a part of the commitment we wanted to make to each other."

As much as she wanted to marry Bill, Marcia knew that if her children strongly objected she couldn't go ahead with her plans. She knew they liked Bill a great deal and were comfortable with him, but she wasn't certain how they would feel about him as a stepfather or as her husband.

Bill and Marcia broached the topic with the children at dinner one evening. Bill asked the children to listen carefully to everything he had to say before responding. Then he told them about his desire to marry their mother, why he thought they would make a good couple, and why he believed they would all be a good family. Marcia watched each of their faces carefully:

> "I watched for the slightest indication of emotion and was very anxious to spot any signs of approval. They each listened attentively to him. And as the news sank in, their eyes grew wide with surprise and each of their faces slowly broke into a full and happy smile. A surge of joy rushed over me. A miracle had taken place—the birth of a family!"

THE STEPFAMILY AS FULFILLMENT

Marcia's joy was rooted in the realization of her dream to have a complete and secure family. This dream had been shattered by the breakup of her first marriage. Now hope flourished anew for her. Most couples who remarry share that dream. Like Marcia, they enter the second union with the hope and determination of making it successful. They are optimistic about the possibilities of a fresh start and of avoiding those problems that doomed their previous marriages. And, for some of them, it will happen.

A few years ago, we interviewed 351 couples who had been married for fourteen years or longer. We wanted to see what happens in marriages that last and work well. We found that about one in seven of these couples was in a second marriage—good news, we think, for those who wonder whether a second marriage can succeed as well as a first one.

So far, it's working for Bill and Marcia. And why not? After all, the children were delighted, and Bill and Marcia were two mature people deeply in love with each other. To be sure, it hasn't been quite as easy or as smooth as they had anticipated. They quickly discovered that their marriage involves all of the challenges of their first marriages plus a number of challenges they didn't face the first time. Nevertheless, it's working.

By "working" we mean that Bill and Marcia have a stable and satisfying family life. They have dealt successfully with a number of problems that can be vexing for stepfamilies. For example, Marcia's children really struggled with the issue of what to call Bill. They felt disloyal to their father when they thought of calling Bill "Dad." So, for now, they call him "Bill." Bill and Marcia have also grappled with the role that he plays in the discipline of the children—a common difficulty in many stepfamilies. Their solution (although it is one that doesn't work in every situation) is that they jointly handle all disciplinary matters.

"It's been tough at times," Marcia admits. "New problems continue to crop up. But after four years, we are truly a family. I thank God that my children live in a home with both a mother and a father and that I have a loving husband."

Will Bill and Marcia live happily ever after? If happily ever after means every moment will be bliss, the answer is no. If happily ever after means they will face up to and work through the difficult times and maintain their commitment to each other and their children, the answer is hopefully. It can be done. Others have done it. But great care, commitment, and faith are required. As Bill and Marcia have already discovered, the challenges facing stepfamilies are generally more severe than those facing families with two biological parents.

THE STEPFAMILY AS FAILURE

Don and Mary Lou illustrate the severity of the challenges to have a successful stepfamiliy. In some ways, their story resembles that of Bill and Marcia. They married with high expectations. They believed they would find the fulfilling marital and family life that had eluded them in their first marriages. Don had no children, but Mary Lou brought her ten-year-old son and thirteen-year-old daughter to the union. Unlike Bill and Marcia, however, Don and Mary Lou were on the verge of divorce within a year.

When Don and Mary Lou came to us, all their conflicts involved the children. Among other things, Mary Lou claimed that Don verbally abused the children. Don insisted that he had never abused them:

> "What she's talking about is discipline. Like one day when Teddy didn't do his homework, I told him he couldn't watch TV until it was done. I found him later in our bedroom, watching a program with Mary Lou. I asked him what he was doing and told him to get out of the room and do his homework."

Mary Lou disagreed with Don's version. She recalled the incident as involving more verbal abuse, as involving Don saying things that made his stepson feel worthless and unwanted.

> "Don tries to control us," Mary Lou complained. "One day Teddy's teacher called from school and said she was returning our call. She asked if I was the one who had called her. Don heard what I was saying and took the phone from me. Then he talked to the teacher about my son. I didn't even know what was going on. I was absolutely clueless. When he hung up, Don told me he had talked at length with Teddy's teacher during a recent parents' night at school, and they had decided on some specific ways to handle him. He had telephoned her to check up on Teddy's progress. I was furious. This is my child and I didn't even know what was going on his life."

Don shook his head. "But we agreed," he pointed out, "that since you couldn't be in two places at the same time on parent's night, I would talk with Teddy's teacher and you would talk with Tina's teacher. Teddy's teacher was concerned about his performance. She said that he was a very bright boy, but he wasn't doing his work. And so we devised a plan to strengthen his study habits. That's all."

Clearly, Don and Mary Lou had not worked out how they would handle their roles and rules in the stepfamily. We had a number of questions for them that illustrated that deficiency. For example, why hadn't Don told Mary Lou about his conversation with Teddy's teacher and his subsequent call to her? And why did Mary Lou object to Don exercising discipline? They agreed that they had never sat down and talked through how they would deal with the children. We suggested some reading materials for them. We advised them to think about the rules and roles they each would prefer and then come to an agreement about what would be acceptable to each of them. We suggested that at some point they would need to bring Teddy and Tina into the discussion so that everyone clearly understood the new arrangement. And we urged them to meet with us weekly as they worked through the issues that threatened their family.

We'd like to say that this was the beginning of a successful rebuilding process. Unfortunately, we never saw them again. Perhaps they took our counsel to heart and managed to salvage their marriage and their family on their own. Or perhaps they are now one of the grim statistics on second marriages.

And the statistics are grim. The divorce rate is even higher for remarriages than for first marriages and varies by the type of remarriage. If one partner is in a first marriage while the other is in a second, the chances for the marriage lasting are about the same as those in first marriages for both partners. But the chances of divorce go up 50 percent if both partners were previously married, and another 50 percent if both were previously married and one or both bring stepchildren into the remarriage.

In other words, the highest rate of divorce in the nation occurs among those in stepfamilies. To forge a lasting and satisfying marriage and family when stepchildren are involved is the greatest relational challenge people can face.

THE SPECIAL CHALLENGES OF THE STEPFAMILY

If you are in, or about to enter, a stepfamily, you will encounter all of the usual challenges and struggles of family life. In addition, you will experience some special challenges—challenges we will deal with in each of the following chapters. The challenges we will examine are those identified by therapists and family experts, as well as by the people who have actually experienced these challenges—members of stepfamilies.

First, you face the challenge of loss. Stepfamily life is built upon loss, including the loss of the original family, of identity, hopes, dreams, and a shared history. Even if you have worked through the pain of failure and betrayal, your children may continue to have feelings of loss and a sense of disruption for many years.

Second, you confront the challenge of adjustment. People often enter stepfamilies with a sense of relief and joyous anticipation that they are going to have a normal family life again. Their bright expectations may be severely diminished when they hit the wall of reality. Maybe you have already experienced this—when your children told you they didn't feel as close to your spouse as they do to their biological parent. Or when your spouse did or said something that reminded you of your ex. Such moments will remind you that your new family is not Edenic but a daunting challenge.

Third, you face the challenge of maintaining personal identity. When you answer the question of who you are, your family roles and routines must be an important part of the answer. Now, however, you are part of a new family and, to some extent, this also makes you a new person. Your challenge is to work with other family members to establish a personal identity that is consistent with God's calling and comfortable for you and other family members.

The fourth challenge is that of family identity. It is the question of who we are. If you think the answer should be obvious, consider such things as the vexing problem of allocating time and family members to all the claimants at Thanksgiving and Christmas. Or the problem of how children should address a new set of grandparents. Or whether Aunt Sarah, the sister of your ex-spouse, should still have your children stay with her for a week each summer. In terms of what it means to be a family, people are forced to decide who's in and who's out. Who gets priority if more people are making requests or demands than you can possibly respond to?

A fifth challenge involves loyalty conflicts. How do your children deal with their feelings for their absent parent and the grandparents on that side? Children are particularly likely to struggle with loyalty conflicts. But you may have some as well. How much responsibility do you have for your ex-spouse's family? These questions illustrate that, even when marriages fail, there are often close ties that have been fashioned with others in the ex-spouse's family. Is it being disloyal to your new family to continue to maintain some of those ties?

Your sixth challenge deals with your feelings about, and your relationship with, your ex-spouse. Most parents in stepfamilies have some contact with ex-spouses, even if it only occurs at the time when children are shared in joint custody arrangements. In addition, there may be emotional ties—positive or negative—that still exist. Next to stepparenting, your dealings with, and your feelings about, your ex-spouse are probably the most critical challenges you face.

Seventh, there is the challenge of resources. We don't know any couples who have all the spare time, all the extra money, and all the excess energy they would like. But if time, money, and energy are at a premium for others, they are even more so for stepfamilies. Time use is complicated by joint custody or visitation arrangements. Money may be tight because of the terms of settlement of one or both divorces. And energy may be consumed in great gulps by all of the above. How can you be a good steward of your resources so that you can realize your dream of a "normal" family life?

The most difficult of all the challenges you are likely to encounter is that of being a stepparent. It can be a tough job. And discipline is likely to be the thorniest stepparenting issue. It can be painful to discipline your natural child; it can feel like you're walking through a mine field to discipline your stepchild. Feelings for the stepchild are also challenging. If it is difficult at times to love your natural child, as most parents acknowledge, how do you handle feelings of despair and disgust when a stepchild is behaving obnoxiously?

The final challenge is that of marital intimacy: in view of all the challenges and demands of stepfamily life, how do you continue to build and strengthen your marriage? Your own stable marriage will be one of the best gifts you can give your children and your stepchildren. It will also be one of the best weapons you have against stepfamily disintegration.

CHRISTIAN TOOLS FOR BUILDING A STEPFAMILY THAT WORKS

If you're feeling a bit bleak or depressed after reviewing the challenges, we encourage you to cheer up. To paraphrase the words of Jesus, in the stepfamily you shall have tribulation. But be of good cheer. For he has overcome the world, and he can enable you to meet and to master every stepfamily challenge. In this book, you will meet a number of Christian stepfamilies who have worked through the challenges and achieved the dream of a secure and satisfying family life. You'll read about their failures and also about their successes. Their low points will encourage you when you are struggling. Their successes will remind you that God does empower his people to overcome.

We will set these experiences of Christian stepfamilies in the context of the biblical teachings they used to meet their personal challenges. And these families found that a number of biblical teachings were crucially important in dealing with the challenges.

In this book, we offer you a number of tools: an understanding of the challenges of stepfamily life as identified by therapists and social scientists; some biblical teachings that address the challenges; and the experiences of stepfamilies that demonstrate how the challenges can be met successfully. With these tools in hand, you can stand with confidence as you confront the stepfamily challenges. These tools will help you to master each challenge as you work with your spouse to create a stable, satisfying, and happy stepfamily.

A Tough Way To Begin
The Challenge of Loss

Happiness is not built upon the foundation of someone else's pain. Yet, in a real sense, that is the way stepfamily life begins. It is an effort to capture the fulfillment of family life, but an effort that grows out of the painful disintegration of at least one and, often two, previous families. The initial challenge facing all stepfamilies is that they originate in loss. The first family (or families) has been shattered through divorce or death, and the loss has been great. Through remarriage, the birth of the new family underscores the finality of what has been lost and, at least for a time, can renew or intensify the pain.

It's vital to the health of your stepfamily that you recognize these experiences of loss and deal with the feelings of anger, guilt, and depression that often generate. If such feelings strike you, your child or stepchild, or your spouse, you'll want to deal with them appropriately—as the aftereffects of loss, not as signs that the stepfamily isn't working. Let's look at the various kinds of losses involved and then at some ways people in stepfamilies are successfully dealing with them.

WHAT THE CHILDREN LOST

Typically, each person in the stepfamily has endured multiple and somewhat unique losses. Think first about the children. They suffer some or all of the following losses when their family is disrupted by a divorce and parents remarry:

1) Loss of a parent. Joint custody or regular visitation can lessen, but they do not eliminate, this sense of loss. As Anne, an introspective 12-year-old with a new stepfather, put it:

> "I was nine when my parents divorced. Even though I hated their arguments, I still didn't want my dad to leave. My sister and I have spent every other weekend with him since the divorce, and we have had some really good times. But it still isn't the same as having him home all the time."

2) Loss of time with the custodial parent. For the parent, remarriage means that "we are a complete family again." But children may see it differently; they now have to share mom or dad with their new stepparent. The stepparent is getting some of the time and attention that had previously been reserved for them. With one parent gone from their home, and the other parent involved with a new partner, the children may feel they have been pushed to the edge of both parents' lives.

3) Loss of hope that their parents will reunite. The remarriage of a divorced parent can be especially distressing for children, who may cling to the hope that their parents will get back together one day. Listen again to Anne:

> "Mom began dating Dan about one year ago. My sister and I liked him from the very beginning. He was fun and made Mom laugh a lot. I was excited, at first, when Mom decided to marry Dan. I was going to be in the wedding and that sounded great. But then I began to realize that if Mom married Dan, she and Dad would never get back together again. And that really made me sad."

4) Loss of stability and security. We all need stability and security. For a child, to be stable and secure means to look at their parents and see two people who can be counted on for protection, guidance, and nurture in the face of the uncertainties of life. In divorce, the parents themselves have become one of the uncertainties. They can no longer be relied on to provide a stable, nurturing home.

5) Loss of the familiar. Children also get a sense of stability and security from being in familiar surroundings—the same house, the same neighborhood, the same school, the same friends. We all feel comfortable and at ease when we are surrounded by the familiar. Anne pointed out that one of the troublesome aspects of her mother's marriage to Dan was moving from their home:

> "Dan didn't want to live in the same house where my dad and mom had lived together. So we moved to a new place. For me that meant a new school and losing my old friends. It was as hard for me as the divorce."

6) Loss of marital optimism. "My parents divorced. I don't intend to do that. I may never marry. And if I do, I'll never put my kids through the pain of divorce." Again and again we have heard such statements from young people who have anxiety about getting married. They think about the disruption of their parents' marriage and think, "This can happen to me too." Unlike those who come into marriage with the expectation that, like their parents, they will be married for life, the children of divorce can be apprehensive about their own chances for marital success.

WHAT THE PARENT LOST

If you're a custodial parent, you probably thought more about what you were gaining, rather than what you were losing, when you remarried. And there are gains. But, like your children and like noncustodial parents, you have also experienced a number of losses that could affect your new family:

l) Loss of a spouse. True, you have gained a spouse. But you have also lost one. And it is perilous to try to build a new marriage if you haven't fully worked through your grief over losing your first spouse—a problem that we'll deal with in detail in chapter 7.

2) Financial loss. We have listened to both men and women who are struggling with financial problems following divorce. Women, however, are particularly vulnerable. Studies of divorced women report drops in household income of up to 30 percent in the first year after divorce. Many women fall below the poverty line for the first time in their lives, and many are bitter about their situation. As Martha, now remarried, put it:

> "The court ordered my ex-husband to pay child support. I got about two months of it. Then he just stopped. He moved to a different state, so I had no recourse. I had to move back in with my parents. It was humiliating and very stressful. I hated making them pay for his lack of responsibility. Anyway, I fell so far behind, that I'm still paying off debts."

3) Loss of confidence. No one goes into marriage expecting divorce. And Christians are particularly likely to feel like they have united with each other for life. When this doesn't happen and their marriages break up, they are likely to lose confidence in their capacity to build lasting unions. As a result, many people enter second marriages with some anxiety. In other words, the confident hope with which they entered the first marriage is likely to be tinged with apprehension. No one wants to go through the pain of another divorce, and no one wants to put children through the pain of another disruption.

4) Loss of time with children. If you're the custodial parent, you may grieve over the loss of time with your children when they spend every other weekend with your ex-spouse. If you're not the custodial parent, you may grieve over the limited hours you now have with your children. Sandra has custody of her three children, but they spend two weekends every month and part of the summer with their father. The arrangement gives Sandra some valuable time for working at her second marriage with Ken, but she still feels the loss:

> "I like having the time with Ken when the kids are with their father. But I really miss them. Especially during the summer when they're gone for weeks at a time. The strange thing is, I missed them even more after Ken and I married. I remember that first weekend they went to their father's after we were married. I kept thinking that we were finally a family again, and all of a sudden we weren't a family. They were only gone for the weekend, but I felt like crying most of the time."

5) Loss of control. There are two ways in which you may lose a certain amount of control. First, you lose some control over your schedule. You are no longer free to schedule family activities without taking into account the children's time with your ex-spouse. It's not at all unusual for ex-spouses to find themselves in a heated argument because one wants the other to give up a scheduled visit with the children for some reason.

Second, you lose some control over your children. If you have custody, your ex-spouse may do things with, say things to, or buy things for your children of which you disapprove. Your ex-spouse may influence your children in ways that are bothersome to you. And if you don't have custody, the problem can be even more acute. Gary is the father of two sons by his first marriage and a daughter by his second. When he divorced, his first wife got custody of the children. Gary's problems with his sons have been ongoing:

> "My ex-wife drives me crazy with the way she deals with our sons. My oldest boy is now dating. Would you believe that on the very first time he went out on a date, she gave him a box of condoms? When I try to talk to him about abstinence before marriage, he just shrugs and says that his mother tells him it's okay as long as he has safe sex."

Understandably, Gary has mourned the loss of control over his sons for all of the twelve years since his divorce.

WHAT THE STEPPARENT LOST

If you're a stepparent who was previously married, you have also lost a spouse. And, like your new partner, you may have lost some confidence and suffered some financial loss. In addition, you are likely to feel other losses:

1) Loss of a honeymoon period of marriage. The honeymoon period of marriage is not simply the trip you take after the marriage service. It is also that unique time when you can devote exclusive attention to each other and experience each other in an intense way. It is a time when two people adjust to living with each other, learn each other's idiosyncrasies, negotiate roles, and develop a sense of being "one flesh." The importance of this period is affirmed in the Old Testament law: "When a man is newly married, he shall not go out with the army or be charged with any related duty. He shall be free at home one year, to be happy with the wife whom he has married" (Deuteronomy 24:5).

The stepparent is more likely than the biological parent to feel this loss. In a real sense, the stepparent is trying to adjust to two new families at once—the family formed with the new spouse and the family that includes the stepchildren. As Sandra's husband, Ken, noted:

> "My stepchildren are wonderful kids. I didn't have kids in my first marriage, so I was really looking forward to having a family. But I have to admit that I really missed not having a year or two alone with Sandra. Having the kids around makes everything a little bit harder. You're just not as free to really get to know each other well."

2) Loss of freedom. After a few months, Ken realized another loss in his life:

> "It was seven years after my divorce that I met Sandra. I was pretty satisfied with my life. But I realized that this was my chance to have something I had always wanted—a family. An instant fam-

ily at that. Don't misunderstand. I wouldn't give up this family for anything. But there are times when I miss the freedom I used to have. A family is a heavy responsibility. I can understand now why some people say that the empty nest is like a second honeymoon."

Ken appreciates his new family. He also intensely feels the responsibilities of parenting. When those responsibilities become particularly burdensome, he remembers the comparatively easy time he had before marriage and realizes the freedom he has lost.

3) Loss of parenting experiences. Ken recognized another loss one day when he and Sandra had the children at the park. They saw a couple with an infant sitting on a bench. The father was playing with his child, while the mother watched with a smile. Ken suddenly felt a pang of regret that he had never experienced the joy of having a baby. He had three stepchildren, but there was a part of each of their lives that he had completely missed:

> "I watched that couple and wondered what it would be like to have a baby. I wished that Sandra and I had met when the kids were even younger, so I could have had more time with them in their earlier years. They all call me Ken. That's okay. I understand. But since that day at the park, I've thought how great it would be to have one child who never knew any father except me and would call me 'Dad.'"

As you think about all the losses involved in stepfamily life, you can understand why the stepfamily is so challenging. You don't have merely the normal—and normally difficult—tasks of other families; you also have to deal with all the losses.

HOW LOSSES AFFECT YOU

Typically, we react to losses with some degree of grief, guilt, anger, and depression. Sandra felt grief when her children went to visit their father. Anne grieved when her parents divorced, and again when her mother talked about remarriage and she realized that the divorce was permanent. Keep in mind that Anne grieved even though she disliked her parents' frequent and intense arguments. Whenever we lose an intimate relationship, even one that is troublesome, we are likely to grieve over the loss.

Guilt is also common. Gary's younger son was six when his parents told him about their upcoming divorce. "When we told him," Gary recalls, "I remember him starting to cry and telling us that he would never be bad again if only we would stay together." The son was already feeling what many children of divorce experience—guilt arising out of the sense that he was somehow to blame.

The son has also had a difficult time in school and a troubled relationship with Gary ever since the divorce. Gary has tried to stay involved in his son's life and to provide him with the assurance of his love. His son, however, remains anxious and troubled. Not surprisingly, Gary feels guilty about subjecting his son to such feelings and about his role in the failure of the marriage.

Anger usually erupts at some point after a loss. Children may be angry at parents for divorcing or angry at a stepparent for making the breakup irreparable. Adults feel anger towards ex-spouses for various reasons, such as Gary's anger at his ex-wife for the way she is raising his sons, and Martha's anger at her ex-husband for reneging on his financial responsibilities. If your ex initiated the divorce, you may be angry at him or her for breaking up the marriage. If you initiated the divorce, you might be angry at your ex for behaving in a way that forced you to take such action. Hopefully, most people get beyond such anger before they marry again. But even then there can be recurring episodes when your new spouse does something that reminds you of your ex or when a problem of stepfamily life is particularly stressful.

Most people also experience some depression after a loss. Anne said she felt sad when she realized her parents would never get together again. Actually, as she talked about it, it sounded more like mild depression because it affected her eating and sleeping habits.

Ken got depressed when he realized he would never have the experience of parenting a baby of his own. Gary sometimes is depressed over the state of his sons and his loss of control in their lives.

Grief, guilt, anger, and depression are not pleasant companions. But if you're experiencing any of them, the good news is that you are not abnormal—on the contrary, you are quite typical—and you can deal effectively with them. There are ways, as we shall see shortly, to cope with our losses. And it is important to cope effectively with them, because they affect your marriage as well as your personal well-being.

HOW LOSSES AFFECT YOUR RELATIONSHIP

If grief, guilt, anger, and depression are unpleasant companions for individuals, they can also be troublesome for your marriage. First, negative emotions take the joyous edge off the marital relationship. To be sure, one of the aspects of married life is sharing one another's burdens. But there will be plenty of those without the additional burdens that grow out of the losses discussed above. In other words, every couple has to deal with times when one or both partners is feeling emotionally distraught, but couples in stepfamilies are likely to have more of these times.

Second, the problem of negative emotions may be compounded for those in stepfamilies because they don't recognize, or don't want to talk about, their source. All of us feel distressed or "below par" at times without fully understanding why. But even if you understand that the source of your distress is related to one or more of the losses you have experienced, you may not want to talk about it with your spouse. Perhaps your spouse is weary of hearing about your first marriage, or perhaps you just don't like thinking about the painful past. You may prefer to get on with this life, this family, and forget the things that are behind.

The problem is, when you are clearly distressed but not saying why, your spouse will assume some basis for your mood. And the thing that occurs first to most people is, "you're upset with me." It's an erroneous assumption, but it's frequently made, and it always detracts from the quality of your relationship.

Losses can detract both from your personal well-being and from the quality of your marriage. Let's see how you can minimize or eliminate the negative effects of those losses.

HOW TO DEAL WITH LOSSES

In working with numerous stepfamilies, we have found that an effective starting place for dealing with losses is God's promise that in all things he is at work for our good (Romans 8:28). This promise is neither a simple nor a shortcut way to deal with loss. But it is essential for all members of the stepfamily to learn to define both their past and their present in terms of God's ongoing work. In effect, the promise of God says to you, "Yes, you have suffered a painful loss. But I am going to heal that hurt and work for your good in all of this." Your focus now changes from "I have lost something good" to "In spite of my loss, God is leading me into something good."

Once you accept that promise, the question is no longer why did we have to suffer such losses? Now the question becomes, what needs to happen, what can we do, to deal with the losses and get on with the task of building a strong family life? The following are some practical steps that worked for Ken and Sandra that we also recommend for your consideration. We urge you to think about each of them and use, or adapt to your situation, as many as you can (and do the same, incidentally, for all other suggestions we will offer in this book).

l) Have a family meeting in which you discuss the various losses that each family member has experienced or is experiencing. This gives every family member the chance to not only understand each other, but to clarify and talk about his or her own sense of loss as well. Begin the meeting by reminding each other that you have not gathered to deny the losses or, for that matter, to deal with them in this meeting. You only want to give each family member a chance to talk about them.

Although this process is not designed to overcome the sense of loss, it can have a therapeutic effect. As Ken recalled about such a family meeting:

> "Even though I knew Sandra and the kids well, we were all a bit uneasy in the first months of our marriage. It was Sandra's idea to have the meeting. And she gave us a good example of what we were to do. She began by telling us that she was very happy about our marriage and about us all being a family now. But she knew we were going to go through some tough times, because each of us had lost some things over the past few years. She wanted us to talk about them so that we could understand and help each other as much as possible."

Sandra told about how her dream of marrying for a lifetime had ended with her divorce. She talked about her sense of loss each time the kids went to visit their father. She said that even though she loved Ken very much and was usually confident of them being together for the rest of their lives, she had periods of anxiety because she could no longer assume that even this marriage was totally secure.

Ken and each of the children then took turns telling about the things they felt they had lost. Following that, they began to ask each other questions: "Did you? . . ." "Do you ever feel? . . ." "Do you think? . . ."

After the meeting, Ken and Sandra felt a fresh breath of life in their family. For one thing, none of them had to pretend that they were free of all hurt. God cannot heal our hurts if we refuse to acknowledge them. For another thing, they all now shared each other's burdens as each realized that "I'm not the only one hurting. We all have our hurts."

2) *Allow each other to grieve the losses.* A woman told us that in the family in which she grew up, negative emotions were not allowed. As "good Christians," they were always to be cheerful. If she got angry, she was sent to her room until she could resume a cheerful demeanor. Her experience is an extreme example of people trying to be Christian by denying all problems. A less extreme example is the stepmother who told us:

> "At one point I thought my whole existence was going down in angry flames—my marriage, my family, and my life. I thought about going to a twelve-step group at our church, but I hesitated because I didn't want to let others know about my problems. I was embarrassed as a Christian to be in such serious trouble. I thought I ought to be able to handle any problem."

Where do such notions come from? Certainly not from Jesus, who wept and got angry, and who even despaired over the slow spiritual development of his disciples. Certainly not from Paul, who wrote about his anger and his agony over the churches. At any rate, it is important to allow each other to grieve over losses. And, as Ken discovered, the family meeting enables each of you to do this:

> "Before the meeting, if one of us got angry or seemed down, the others would urge that person to 'get with it', to work with the rest of us to make this a good family. After the meeting, we became sensitive to the fact that anger or depression could be related to the loss. One night when I was feeling low, Sandra asked me about it. At first, I said it was nothing. She said that if it was something to do with our family, she needed to know about it. So I told her that I was feeling down because the responsibilities of the family just got overwhelming at times. She put her arm around me, told me she knew that I had given up a lot to marry her and be a father to her children, and she loved me deeply for it. What a great moment that was for me."

Sandra didn't try to lift Ken out of his low spirits. She didn't berate him for it. She understood that he was dealing with a sense of loss. And she simply shared his burden and expressed her love.

3) *Give special attention to each family member in turn.* One of the ways that God works for our good is to inspire us to work for the good of each other. And one of the ways to work for someone else's good is to do something special for them. It's also a way to ease the hurt of loss, because it puts the emphasis on what you have gained by the new arrangement.

The way Ken and Sandra have done this is to plan something special each month for one member of the family. When it's Ken or Sandra's turn to be special, the other one works with the children to plan the special event. The special events need not be complex or expensive. They are merely a way of affirming each family member as a special person and the family itself as a special group of which they are a part. Ken described how one such special event affected his oldest stepdaughter:

> "Sherry has had the toughest time with her parents' divorce and adjusting to stepfamily life. When we first proposed the idea of doing something special each month for someone, she rolled her eyes and gave us a look of disdain that she has perfected since she became a teenager. But we insisted that we were going to do it. When her turn came, she said she really didn't want anything special for herself. But we pressed her, and so did her brother and sister. So she finally agreed. It would be special for her, she said, to spend the weekend with her friend. We told her we would consider that at another time, but we had agreed that the special thing would involve the whole family. Well, she said, if the whole family had to be involved, she'd prefer to do it out of town."

Ken and Sandra would not allow their idea to be frustrated by Sherry's lack of cooperation. They told her they would accept her condition, and that they and her brother and sister would plan a special surprise for her that would take place out of town. Sherry looked startled by this response, but said nothing.

> "I don't think she believed we would actually do anything. But we put our heads together and came up with a plan. We would not tell Sherry where she was going, but the next Saturday we

would take her to a horse farm that was about 65 miles from our home. She loved to ride, but had little opportunity to do so. We took a picnic lunch so she could spend most of the day riding once we got there."

Sherry's special day turned out to be just that—very special for every member of the family. When they arrived at the farm and told Sherry of the plan, she got teary-eyed. She thanked and hugged them. To Ken's dismay (unlike Sherry, he hates riding horses), they stayed the entire day:

> "I had a sore backside for days. But every time I felt the soreness, I remembered the look on Sherry's face. I think it was a real turning point for our family."

Ken and Sandra continue to face the challenges that come to all stepfamilies. But affirming the fact that God is at work in them for their good, having the family meeting to air their losses, allowing each other to grieve those losses, and working to make each family member a special person in a special family has set them on a healthy course. The same techniques can work for you.

Not an Ordinary Family
The Challenge of Adjustment

Meg and Tom had been married only two weeks when they realized they were in for some rough times. It was Tom's first marriage and Meg's second marriage. Meg's first husband had been killed in an automobile accident shortly after the birth of their third son. Meg had several difficult years raising the boys without a father and working full-time as a third grade teacher. When she fell in love and married Tom, she felt that the difficult years were behind her. "Was I ever in for a surprise," Meg told us:

> "Tom and the boys had gotten along so well before the wedding, I thought it could only get better after we were married. I quickly realized this wasn't to be. I expected that Tom would automatically become the boys' father, and that they would welcome him as their dad. But this is not what happened at all."

To her dismay, Meg discovered that her sons' seemingly easy acceptance of Tom turned into resistance and resentment when Tom tried to exercise discipline. The oldest son, Jimmy, had argued with a boy at school and had torn his notebook. When Tom was informed of the incident by the principal, he scolded Jimmy and told him that he could not watch television for one week. Jimmy looked startled and replied angrily, "Mom didn't say that. You can't tell me what to do." This infuriated Tom, and he and Jimmy quickly got into an argument.

It was the beginning of a lengthy struggle to establish a workable stepfamily. Clearly, they had a problem. But Jimmy was not the problem. And Tom was not the problem. The problem was that they began their life together with an unrealistic expectation—that they would function from the beginning in the same way as a biological family. Tom and Meg were at the "fantasy stage" of stepfamily life, the stage at which one or more of the family members have unrealistic expectations about how their life together will be.

The challenge of adjustment is to shed unrealistic expectations and replace them with realistic ones. First, let's look at some of the common unrealistic expectations that stepfamily members have in the fantasy stage.

FANTASY EXPECTATIONS

Fantasy expectations reflect our love of fairy-tale story endings— they all lived happily ever after. You no doubt would like to have a fairy-story ending to your own life. Ironically, the more you cling to fantasy expectations the less likely you are to experience the happiness embodied in those expectations. To see the truth of this, consider some of the common fantasy expectations:

1) We will be a "normal" family again. To be blunt, no you won't. Not, at any rate, if by "normal" you mean that "step" will disappear from your vocabulary and each of you will relate to the others as though there never was another parent or spouse involved with your family.

Of course, everyone craves a normal family. It's understandable that many people enter stepfamily life with this expectation. But it's a potential time bomb. You will find yourself deeply distressed every time something happens that reminds you that you are not a normal family. And, like Ruth, a medical technician whose stepfamily failed, you may find yourself sabotaging your family by your efforts to normalize it.

After seven years of frustration, Ruth's marriage broke up. She had married Frank, who brought two adolescent children with him from his first marriage. Frank's first wife had abandoned him and the children in an effort to find herself. Ruth was determined they would have a normal family; that she would be a mother and not a stepmother. She was determined to make Frank feel secure, for she knew his apprehensions about being abandoned again.

What this meant for her was, for the most part, that she denied her personal needs and lived for her family. She tried hard to please her stepchildren, catering to their every desire, encouraging them to call her "Mom," and generally adorning their lives with permissiveness. When they criticized her or failed to appreciate her efforts, she was devastated. When they took advantage of her kindness, she tried to ignore it. When they made cutting remarks about her, she tried to laugh them off.

Her marriage was also frustrating. When Frank expressed jealousy over business lunches with a male colleague, she stopped having them. When he said he was tired, she took over his share of the household chores. When he expressed concern over her work schedule, she asked for reduced hours.

For seven years she struggled. In the end, she was defeated by her own expectations. In her determination to have a normal family life, she acted abnormally and virtually guaranteed they would never even come close to her fantasy of normality.

2) We will love each other. It depends on what you mean by love (we will discuss below how biblical love—agape—is a realistic expectation). Ruth doggedly tried to create love in her family. By love she meant feelings of warmth, affection, and connectedness. At times, however, Ruth felt not just a lack of love but a decided dislike for her stepchildren. This, in turn, made her feel guilty, further compounding her relationship with them.

Again, of course, we all prefer to be in a family in which feelings of love abound. But that kind of love is not something you can command. Try as she might, Ruth could not force herself to feel warmth and affection toward her stepchildren. Try as she might, she could not make herself feel connected to them as though they were her own. And the insistent effort to do so led to burn out in her relationships with her stepchildren and in her marriage.

3) We will not have the problems that other stepfamilies have. We'd all like to think we're different. Ruth was certain that she was different. She was, after all, a decent person. She attended church. She had committed herself to love a man and to love his children as though they were her own. Such qualities, she admits, made her think she should be exempt from the problems she knew other stepfamilies faced:

> "I knew of stepfamilies where the stepmother clearly did not regard the children as her own. And one of my friends admitted to me that from the first day of her marriage she knew she would not endure misery, and would bail out if it didn't work. I wasn't like that. And Frank wasn't like those fathers who let the stepmother take over all of the childrearing tasks.
>
> "You see why I thought we were different? And why I thought we wouldn't have the same problems that we saw in other stepfamilies? I think these expectations made our problems all the worse. It was as if I had somehow been betrayed by it all."

4) And so on and so on. People bring many additional kinds of fantasy expectations into a stepfamily. Here are a few that we have heard:

> "This family will be easier because we're older and more mature." (No. A stepfamily is unlikely to ever be easier than a family with two biological parents.)

"Our love for each other will enable us to overcome any problems with the children." (Wouldn't that be nice? If it were so, the rate of breakup would not be so high.)

"Because we love each other so much, the children will just have to love us both." (Why? Do you like all of your children's friends? Do they like all of yours? What if they see your love for each other as a threat rather than a good thing?)

"Their real father is out of the picture completely, so we won't have to deal with that issue." (This is unrealistic. Even if he is deceased, he is still their biological father, and you ignore that at your peril and the peril of your family.)

"We won't have custody of the children. They'll only be here every other weekend, so I don't expect them to be a major problem." (Try it for a year, then let us know if you still believe this. The weekends they spend with you are not the only time they will affect you.)

"My daughter will be so much better off when she has a father." (Hopefully, in time, she will be better off. But don't be dismayed if, initially, she fights the prospect and even acts as though you have ruined her life.)

THE DANGERS OF FANTASY EXPECTATIONS

As Ruth explains, fantasy expectations are dangerous because they lead you to behave in ways that can come back to haunt you. At the least, you may be distressed when your fantasies are not fulfilled. But worse, you may find yourself in another failed marriage.

For example, if you believe that you are going to have a normal family, you might decide that the children should call their stepparent "Mom" or "Dad." How else can you have a normal family?

But this can be a mistake with children of almost any age. A woman whose widowed father remarried told us about her feelings when her father startled her one day with a request:

> "It just came out of the blue as far as I was concerned. They hadn't been married very long, and I was visiting them with my son and daughter. Out of the blue, my dad told my children to call his wife 'Grandma.' Then he looked at me and said, only half-jokingly, 'And you can call her "Mom" if you want.'
>
> "I was furious. When I got home, I told my children they didn't have to call her 'Grandma.' I reminded them of the grandma they had who loved them very much. I told them to be polite and nice, and that they would learn to love their grandfather's new wife. But they could call her whatever was comfortable for them."

Her father was well-meaning. He wanted his wife to be fully accepted as a member of the family. But his expectation that this could happen immediately was a fantasy. And it led him to act in a way that complicated, rather than helped, the process of acceptance.

There is another side to the problem. Fantasy expectations not only lead you to act in counterproductive ways, they also divert your attention from the real challenges you face. Yet people often cling to unrealistic expectations because they seem to answer a strong personal need. For example, Tom—who we met at the beginning of this chapter—desperately wanted a family. Because of a physical condition, however, it was unlikely that he would ever have children of his own. When he met Meg, he suddenly saw not only a woman he found very attractive, but the possibility of a family he wasn't sure he could ever have.

Because of his strong need for a family, Tom ignored the challenges he would face as a stepfather. He dreamed about the times when he would play ball with the boys. He envisioned them all camping together, and he and the boys doing "guy things." But he hadn't carefully thought through ways to develop the kind of parental relationship he wanted with his stepsons. In fact, he and Meg had never even discussed issues like discipline before they married.

When the first confrontation with Jimmy occurred, Tom reacted more angrily than the situation warranted because of his punctured fantasies. Instead of thinking about how to come to terms with his role as a stepfather, he was diverted into mourning the assault on his fantasies. He suffered emotional pain and wasted much time and energy before he finally abandoned the fantasies and faced up to the challenges.

CREATING REALISTIC EXPECTATIONS

Does discarding your fantasy expectations mean you are giving up on a rich family life? Not at all. On the contrary, it means you are eliminating significant obstacles to the development of a rich family life. But it isn't enough to get rid of the fantasies. As Jesus pointed out, when you get rid of an unclean spirit, you must fill the emptiness with something good or the "last state" may be "worse than the first" (Luke 11:24-26).

Thus, you need to replace your fantasy expectations with realistic expectations—those that will provide the foundation for building a stepfamily that really works. Here's one way to proceed:

1) Accept the fact that your stepfamily will differ from a family with two biological parents. Put the emphasis on the fact that it will be different, not better or worse, not right or wrong, just different. One of the consequences of accepting this fact is that you won't continue to compare what happens in your family with what happens in families where the two biological parents are present. It is precisely such a comparison that can bring people to the edge of despair, as with Meg:

> "We had disagreements in the home I grew up in, but we always knew that we belonged together. We knew our parents cared

about us, and we knew they had the right to discipline us, even if we didn't like the way they did it. But my boys seem determined not to allow Tom to be a father to them—you can't be a father if you don't discipline."

It is clear that Meg expected her stepfamily to conform to her ideal—the biological family she grew up in. She expected her sons to accept Tom as the disciplinarian simply because he was now her husband and the man in the house. And as long as she held these expectations, the stepfamily lost out by comparison. It wasn't until both Tom and Meg accepted the fact that a stepfamily is a different kind of family that they were able to discard the unrealistic model they had been using and start the task of building a workable family life.

2) As one of your goals, aim for respect rather than affection.
Many stepparents resist this. "I want my stepchildren to love me, and I want to love them" is a typical stance. No one denies the desirability of such a goal. And it's understandable that people prefer to receive the instructions: "Go directly to love. Bypass all difficulties and struggles and proceed directly to love." But love in step-relationships is one of those goals that is more likely to be gained by increments. So, as a first step, strive for respect.

Respect means to acknowledge and appreciate the good qualities that others have. It means to accept the potential for a mutually beneficial relationship with others. Note that we say "others," because respect is needed on all sides. Stepchildren must respect their stepparents, and stepparents must respect their stepchildren. You cannot receive respect if you do not give respect.

Respect is something people can exercise independently of how they feel about another person. For instance, you don't have to like your boss to treat him or her civilly and acknowledge whatever good qualities he or she has. You might prefer a different boss, but you can still treat your boss with respect.

Similarly, stepparents might not particularly like their

stepchildren. Yet a stepparent can still treat those children with respect, if for no other reason than that God loves and wills for them the very best. And stepchildren may not care for their new stepparent. They may prefer someone else, or even no one else. But they can still treat their stepparent with respect, if for no other reason than that they have a Christian responsibility to treat all people with respect. As Paul admonishes, "If it is possible, so far as it depends on you, live peaceably with all" (Romans 12:18). This can only happen among people who treat each other with respect.

We believe the biological parent should take the lead in establishing respect in the stepfamily. Once this respect is established and maintained, a foundation is established for building affection. For example, a mother helped her children eventually achieve feelings of affection for her new husband by insisting on respect from the outset. Her son was twelve and her daughter was ten when she remarried. Her husband, Ted, had been married before but was childless. He was apprehensive about raising children but was willing to make the effort. Before the marriage took place, his wife facilitated the process by telling her children, "Ted is not your father. He doesn't expect you to call him 'Dad' or even to think of him in this way. He will be my husband. And because he is my husband, I expect you to treat him with the same respect with which you treat me." She also told the children they would learn to appreciate Ted's good qualities and that he could add a great deal to their lives.

The children were not completely sold on the idea of a stepfather, but they treated him with respect as their mother taught them. Ten years later, they now regard Ted with deep affection and often turn to him for advice.

There is one caveat to mention. A stepfamily is not different in every way. No child treats his or her parents with respect at all times. Don't expect a child to unfailingly treat a stepparent with respect. There were times when Ted's stepchildren were not civil to him. It helped him to realize they were not always civil to their mother either. It also showed Ted that he and his wife failed at times to show proper respect for the children. Fortunately, they realized that instances of disrespect do not mean the effort has failed, but that the process must involve human fallibility.

3) Practice agape *love.* When you exercise respect, you are already practicing *agape* love. Agape is the most commonly used Greek word for love in the New Testament. When we are directed to love one another, agape is the word most often used. When we are told to love God, or that God loves us, agape is the word that is used.

The Greeks had other words for love, words that referred to sexual love, to love between friends, and to love between family members. The Greeks actually made little use of agape. But it became the predominant term for love in the New Testament.

What's so special about agape? In essence, agape means to act on behalf of the well-being of others independently of how you feel about them. That's the beauty of Christian love—you are not hamstrung in your efforts by your emotions. "I don't feel like it," "I don't like that person," and other such statements are not impregnable barriers to acting in a way that is helpful to someone. The point is, you can't expect someone to feel affection for you just because you are now legally a part of the family. But you can expect to give and receive agape love.

Again, the biological parent is crucial in helping the children learn to practice this kind of love. In part, this involves the willingness to accept a child's feelings of resentment or of dislike or of being mistreated. The response is, "I understand how you feel, and I know you can't help feeling that way. But you can still . . ."

For example, let us imagine a dialogue between a nine-year-old daughter and her mother. In an effort to build their relationship, her stepfather wants to take his stepdaughter on an outing. But she doesn't want to go with him. She doesn't dislike him, but she doesn't think of him as her father and suspects he wants her to be like a daughter to him.

Daughter: "I don't want to go. He isn't my real dad."
Mother: "We know that. But he still would like to take you."
Daughter: "I'm not happy about going, and I won't have a good time. So why does he want me to go?"
Mother: "It's okay if you're not happy, and you can't help it if you don't have a good time. Sometimes we just do things for other people because it's good for them."

This mother is teaching her daughter how to practice agape love. She is teaching her that we are able to act independently of, and even contrary to, our feelings. If the daughter goes, it might be a step forward in her relationship with her stepfather and also a valuable experience in learning how to love.

Of course, the way for children to learn the meaning and value of agape love is to see it practiced by adults. It is worthwhile to occasionally point out to children those instances when you did something for them that you didn't feel like doing at the moment. You might also note that there may be rewards in practicing such love (please don't give the impression that there always will be). For instance, "Yes, I understand you don't want to do this. I felt the same way when I took you to that movie you wanted to see. I was so busy I really didn't want to go. And you know what? I had a great time because I was with you and you enjoyed it so much."

4) *Exercise patience.* You know the old saying, Rome wasn't built in a day and neither is a satisfying stepfamily. And your stepfamily probably won't be built as quickly as you would like. As a stepmother put it, "I expected to have some problems. But I never thought it would take so long to deal with them."

Many stepfamilies find the first two years of the marriage to be the most difficult part, but not the end, of the challenge of adjustment. One of the reasons for the length of the process is that you need to allow children to adjust at their own pace. Perhaps most stepparents have had the experience of wanting to shout at a stepchild when facing a particular issue, "We've been through this time and again. Let's stop this game and move on." That's what we mean by the need for patience. And patience comes more easily if you accept the fact that the process of adjustment may not occur as quickly as you once expected or as quickly as you would like.

It can also help you to be patient if you realize that children are not making a perverse choice in setting a timetable for adjustment. They are only acting in accord with their own feelings, trying to sort through their own struggles and attempting to make their world a livable one. This takes time. And the time it takes varies from one individual to another.

It may help you to exercise patience if you remind yourself that many others have found the initial period of stepfamily life to be rough and nearly unbearable, yet have stuck with it, and have finally emerged with a satisfying family. Angie had a son and a daughter when she married Steve, who had one son. Angie had full custody of her children. Steve had his son on weekends. Initially, Angie recalls, family life was pure chaos every weekend:

> "I got to the point where I could hardly bear the thought of Steve's son arriving. He was the oldest, and I felt like he bullied my son. I both dreaded and resented his coming. And the feelings became so strong that they never went away. War broke out between Steve and me—sometimes it was a cold war and sometimes it was a hot war of words."

Angie finally went to a therapist. She felt unable to cope but hated the thought of a second marriage breaking up. In therapy, she realized that one of her problems was that she believed she ought to feel like a mother toward Steve's son. The therapist encouraged her to try to be just a friend. He also reminded her that building any good relationship is a time-consuming process. "Give it more time," he urged, "and stop expecting a miracle of instant harmony."

She took his advice and it worked. She reports that after a few years, her two children and her stepson are relating to each other as if they were lifelong siblings. And she and her stepson have become good friends.

5) *Expect to be a stepparent—not a parent nor a super-parent.*
We will discuss stepparenting more thoroughly in chapter nine. Here we want to emphasize the importance of being realistic about what you can do if you have stepchildren. This also means accepting what you cannot do. You probably cannot take the place of a child's biological parent. We say "probably" because we have known many cases of children who come to regard a stepparent as "the only father (mother) I know." A bond develops between the stepchild and stepparent that is akin to that of a biological parent and child. You may or may not want that to happen. In either case, you should not expect it to happen. If it does, and if you want it, it will be the delicious frosting on the cake of your stepparenting. But it isn't necessary in order for you to have a meaningful stepparenting experience.

Another thing you cannot do, indeed that you must not do, is try to become a super-parent. We define a superparent as one who tries to relate to a stepchild like Superman related to Lois Lane—always there to rescue her and to fulfill all her needs. Super-parents are always at the beck and call of their stepchildren. They forego their own pleasures and desires in order to try to please their stepchildren. They neglect their marital relationship in order to make the stepchildren happy. They are determined to be loved by their stepchildren, sometimes even to the point of trying to ignore the children's need for limits, rules, and discipline.

The superparent may feel anger, but tries to stifle it. The superparent may experience frustration, but tries to pretend it isn't so. The superparent may be hurt by the stepchild's misbehavior, but acts as though everything is okay.

In a word, super-parents are trying too hard to make everything okay in the stepchild's world. And even in those rare cases where a superparent succeeds in growing a healthy stepchild, the price will be a heavy one. As a stepmother told us, "The children are doing well. But I'm worn down to nothing, and our marriage is a wreck."

Be realistic about what you can and cannot do for any child. You may be called to be a stepparent. You are not called to be your stepchild's god.

6) Keep in mind the difference between stepfamily issues and those that would occur anyway. This is another way of saying, don't blame all your problems and challenges on the stepfamily. If you're realistic, you expect to have some difficult times whether you're part of a stepfamily or not. The temptation is to blame all the problems on the stepfamily, and this makes it even harder to adjust.

For example, when Paul and Emily married, Emily's daughter, Michelle, was just entering adolescence. They had all the usual problems of adjusting to stepfamily life, but also had the typical problems of an adolescent child in the home. Emily and Michelle had always gotten along well but now strains suddenly seemed to develop. They began arguing about everything from Michelle's responsibilities around the house to her desire for more freedom. Michelle blamed Paul for their conflict. And Emily began to believe her daughter because the conflict had started soon after she and Paul married.

Finally, Paul made an important observation:

> "I am not the problem. I know it's harder for you since I've come into your lives. It's harder for me too. [But] it's really hard when you blame me for things that would have happened even if you had never met me. Michelle, you're in a new phase of life—not just because of me, but because you're growing into adulthood. And Emily, you would be having difficulties with Michelle at this point whether I was here or not."

Paul's observation didn't put an end to their struggles. But it put them into perspective and enabled family members to deal more realistically with the challenges they faced. They no longer treat every issue as a stepfamily problem.

7) *Expect to find creative ways to minimize conflict.* Every issue is not inherently a big issue. But every issue can become one. If you expect to be creative and find ways to minimize some of the conflict, you will. We believe that all people are creative. If two people work together, the creativity potential is multiplied. All it takes to be creative is to view an issue as a problem to be solved rather than as a war to be waged and won.

Take, for example, the experience of a stepfamily which included the adolescent children of both partners. The parents decided that the only way to get all of the household tasks done was to require each child to do his or her own laundry. That seemed to be a good solution. But bath towels proved to be a problem. The teenagers argued over who had used the various towels and who should wash them. The parents put their heads together and resolved the issue by color coding the towels used by each family member.

A man told us that one of the more rancorous fights he had in his first marriage was over the toothpaste tube. He hated the way his wife squeezed it from the middle, and she hated the way he rolled it up as he used it. In his second marriage, he once again faced the toothpaste tube challenge—this time with his stepchild as well as his wife. He was determined not to allow such a relatively trivial issue to become an issue of contention. He and his wife creatively solved the problem—they have three tubes of toothpaste, one for each member of the family.

Obviously, all stepfamily problems can't be solved as easily and simply. Some relatively minor issues that turn into major arguments can be avoided with a little creative problem solving. You will have plenty of tough challenges. So conserve your energy by not struggling long and hard over minor issues.

8) *Expect rewards as well as challenges.* It isn't realistic to expect a "happily-ever-after" situation, but you can expect some rewards, even while you're in the midst of struggle. "We know that all things work together for good for those who love God, who are called according to his purpose" (Romans 8:28).

The rewards vary from a sense of being part of a family to developing and refining interpersonal skills. For example, because the challenges are great and relationships complex, stepfamily life can teach you how to negotiate effectively with others. Being part of a stepfamily also may increase the number of people to whom you can turn for guidance and support. Moreover, you may pick up new traditions, new patterns of household functioning, and new interests as a result of the diverse experiences and backgrounds that various members bring to the stepfamily.

Your adjustment will be easier if you focus on the rewards as much as possible. As a stepfather observed:

> "There are times when my stepdaughter won't give me the time of day. But once in a while, she acts like she really could grow to like me. So I try to remind myself that her hostility will eventually go away, and I keep thinking about the times when she seems to appreciate me. I think those times are increasing."

9) *Think of you and your spouse as a team.* This doesn't mean that you each have to address every issue or share equally in the solution of every problem. What it does mean is that you face every challenge as a team, decide what each of you needs to do, and tackle the challenge accordingly. It is unrealistic to expect the biological parent to assume full responsibility for all discipline at all times. It is unrealistic to expect the stepparent to assume total responsibility for forging a close relationship with the stepchildren. In all matters—whether it's the discipline of the children, the demands of a two-career couple, or the distribution of household chores—you need to work together as a team. It's the only way you can successfully adjust to the realities of stepfamily life.

For example, Barbara is having a difficult time adjusting to being a stepmother:

> "I'm trying to cope with my stepson, Mike. He's a teenager, and he treats me as if I don't exist. I know what it's like to deal with a teenage boy. I went through it with my own son, Kent, who's

away at college now. Kent and I had our arguments. Still we each knew where the other stood, and our relationship remained solid. But I can't argue with Mike because he just won't respond to me. And when I try to talk to my husband about the problem, he tells me the 'poor boy' is still suffering from the divorce, and it's something Mike and I need to work out together."

This marriage could be in trouble if Barbara's husband doesn't accept his need to work with her as a team. At this point, he should sit down and discuss the options for handling Mike. This a situation that is crying out for teamwork.

10) Expect adjustment to be an ongoing process. Change is a lifelong process, regardless of whether you are in a stepfamily. But if you are part of a stepfamily, you face additional challenges that often make adjustment seem the constant theme of your life. So don't be dismayed when you successfully negotiate a particular challenge only to find yourself confronting another. For example, you may successfully adjust to being a stepparent, then find yourself facing a whole new set of challenges when your stepchild returns after spending the summer with his or her noncustodial parent.

Similarly, a new baby brings its own set of demands and challenges, some of which are unique when there are already children from another marriage in the home. A woman whose son and husband had formed a close stepfather-stepson relationship was distressed at her son's reaction when his half-brother was born:

"I thought my son might be jealous because we were giving attention to the baby. After all, he had all the attention for five years. I wasn't prepared for how angry he was with my husband. They had gotten along so well. But now it feels like we're back to square one."

What happens in such situations is that the stepchild feels his or her special status in the family—both with the biological parent and the stepparent—is threatened. Think of it from the child's point of view. It's like being hit with two blows at once. Your parent is now going to be giving attention and love to a new baby. Will your parent love you as much? And your stepparent now has his or her own biological child. How could your stepparent ever care as much for you as for his or her own baby? Anger is an understandable reaction to such a sense of loss. It takes a good deal of reassurance and attention from both the parent and the stepparent to enable the child to cope.

You may or may not face such a situation. But you will face ongoing challenges. So expect adjustment to be an ongoing process. This isn't a word of pessimism. It's just a reminder to lean heavily upon the grace of God which is sufficient for your every need—including your need to fashion a stepfamily that is a blessing for each member.

Who Am I?

The Challenge of Personal Identity

When Jack and Stephanie wed, they each brought along two children from previous marriages. They also brought very different experiences of family life from their childhoods. Jack had been raised in a boisterous family of five children where life was disorganized and chaotic. Stephanie, on the other hand, was an only child who grew up in a quiet, organized home. Needless to say, they brought to their marriage very different understandings of what a family should look like.

This was just the tip of the iceberg. Each brought personal experiences of family life from their first marriages. Their children had different experiences in their biological families. So, in effect, here were six people—with diverse sets of family experiences, different notions of what a family ought to be, and various kinds of ties to each other— trying to live in harmony as one family.

Not surprisingly, each floundered as he or she sought to figure out just who each was within this new set of relationships. All of us, at one time or another, struggle with the issue of personal identity. But the question of identity can be particularly difficult to answer for those in stepfamilies.

WHY PERSONAL IDENTITY IS IMPORTANT

What does personal identity mean? In essence, your personal identity is your understanding of who you are—your personality, abilities, moral and spiritual commitments, interpersonal skills, roles, and self-image. Self-image includes such things as whether you see yourself as loving, spiritual, intelligent, lovable, sensitive, liberal or conservative, family- or work-oriented, traditional or novel.

How do you develop an identity? Actually, your identity is shaped to a considerable extent by your roles and your intimate relationships with parents, siblings, extended family members, friends, teachers, pastors, and others. For example, if you identify yourself as a caring person in general and a caring parent in particular, this identity probably stems from your understanding of the parental role, your religious training, and the model of caring you learned from your parents. Perhaps various people have said something or related to you in a way which reinforced the notion that you are a caring person. Even such a simple thing as someone saying "thank you for asking" to you when you inquire about that person's well-being, reminds you that you are a caring person and strengthens this part of your identity.

Because identities are tied up in experiences with others, they change over time. A person close to you (such as a parent or a friend) might express deep gratitude for what you have meant to him or her, thereby enhancing some part of your identity ("I am a devoted child or friend"). Or someone may express admiration for skills that you have never recognized in yourself, thereby adding a new dimension to your identity. A woman told us that she never thought of herself as an intelligent person until she was speaking to her pastor one day and he praised her intelligence. She was startled by his comment. No one in her memory had ever told her she was intelligent. When he explained that he was impressed by her facility with words and her ability to express herself with clarity and insight, she realized that he was not complimenting her to win favor. "He actually believed I was intelligent," she said. And from that day on, her identity had a new dimension.

Personal identity is important because it is an integral part of your well-being. It is far healthier, for example, to see yourself as a competent rather than an inept person. It is healthier if you regard yourself as a delightful person rather than as a bore. And if you wonder whether such positive perspectives are inconsistent with faith, keep in mind the statement by Paul: "I can do all things through him who strengthens me" (Philippians 4:13). In that affirmation, Paul linked his capacity to deal competently with every kind of situation to God's working in his life.

You can see yourself in such terms as competent and delightful because your competence, your attractiveness, and all other positive attributes are given to you and sustained by God. The positive aspects of your identity are not a form of pride, but a celebration of your life in Christ.

There is a second reason why identity is important: people strive to act in ways that are consistent with their identities. If you think of yourself as a caring person, you will strive to be caring in every situation. If you think of yourself as generally competent, you are more open to accepting a leadership position; or, more importantly for our purposes, you are less likely to cave in to the challenges of building a workable stepfamily. If you think of yourself as a delightful person, you will do better at forging good stepfamily relationships than if you think of yourself in negative terms.

Consider this example. Phil is about to become a stepfather. Let's assume that Phil thinks of himself as attractive to his wife but not as someone who relates well to children. He begins his stepfathering with the assumption that he's going to have problems, that the children are not likely to care for him, and that he is unlikely to understand them. As a result, he minimizes his interaction with them and his involvement in decisions about their activities, responsibilities, and discipline.

Now let's view the situation in a different way. Suppose that Phil thinks of himself as able to get along well with children. He begins stepfathering with the assumption that, although there will be problems, the children will grow to care for him in time and he will be able to relate to them in a way that will be mutually rewarding. As a result, he spends time doing special things with and for them and showing them that he both respects and cares about them.

Think about what will happen when Phil has difficulties with his stepchildren. The "first" Phil will see the difficulties as a confirmation that he is "not good with children" and will withdraw further. The "second" Phil will view the difficulties as challenges to the way he thinks of himself and will continue with his efforts to confirm his identity.

It is obvious which Phil has the greater probability of successful stepfathering. Clearly, identity is important in stepfamily life.

THE STEPFAMILY AS A CHALLENGE TO IDENTITY

It's not surprising that identity is greatly challenged when you become part of a stepfamily. A stepfamily forces family members into new roles. It also presents a new set of complex relationships with people who have diverse experiences and differing expectations. Each of them has been part of another family system with different customs, manners, and beliefs. And such matters—from how they celebrate holidays to what they believe about religion, politics, and other matters—play a part in challenging old identities as well as shaping new identities of stepfamily members.

In many ways, stepfamilies force members to rethink their identities. Can you continue to think of yourself as a loving person if you find a stepchild's behavior obnoxious? Can you view yourself as lovable if a stepchild doesn't reciprocate your overtures of love? In what sense are you someone who values traditions if your new family clings to different traditions? Will you remain politically conservative or liberal if your new spouse has a different orientation? What happens to your spiritual commitment if your stepchildren resist going to church with you?

It may help to keep in mind that your identity struggles are also shared by other members of your stepfamily. We spoke earlier about Jack and Stephanie who came from very different family situations. But this was only one of many identity-challenging differences that they brought to their stepfamily. For example:

• Jack's children were seldom ill, but Stephanie's daughter suffered from chronic asthma. Part of Stephanie's identity included being a nurse to her daughter; Jack never thought of his parental role in this way.

• Stephanie's children were honor students; Jack's children were average students. Jack's children had never thought of themselves as intellectually mediocre until they were constantly confronted with their stepsiblings' superior performance.

• Jack was a moderate Republican; Stephanie was a liberal Democrat. Now they each had to reconsider their political perspectives because someone they cared deeply about differed from them.

• Jack handled disagreements by loudly arguing his point; Stephanie avoided conflict when she could. Jack and his children had minimal experience with Stephanie's style, and Stephanie and her children had little experience with Jack's style. And so each had to rethink what kind of person he or she was when disagreements occurred.

• Jack was openly and passionately affectionate; Stephanie was embarrassed with displays of passion in the presence of the children. They both felt challenged in their identities as sexual individuals.

• Jack typically celebrated his children's birthdays with moderation; Stephanie always celebrated with numerous gifts and special parties. Jack felt that Stephanie's practice was extravagant while Stephanie thought Jack's was stingy.

The differences challenged each of their identities: Jack had always thought of himself as caring (was he really too tight?), while Stephanie had always thought of herself as reasonable (was she overly extravagant?).

Of course, such differences occur in biological families as well. Yet the differences are compounded in a stepfamily. Take, for example, Stephanie's discomfort with Jack's displays of affection. For the most part, her uneasiness stemmed from her concern over Jack's children. She knew the importance of children seeing their parents openly express affection for each other. But she also thought she detected looks of embarrassed resistance on the faces of Jack's children—looks that she interpreted (correctly or incorrectly) to mean, "You have stolen our father's love from our mother. When he kisses you, he betrays our mother."

In addition to different experiences and expectations, the various stepfamily roles also pose a challenge to identity. Let's consider what it means to be a spouse, a stepparent, and a stepchild.

1) What does it mean to be a spouse in a stepfamily? Remarriage is a challenge to your spousal identity even without stepchildren. A fundamental task in all marriages is balancing your needs with those of your spouse so that each of you feels fulfilled. In a first marriage, newlyweds can focus on each other and on their relationship. The arrival of children, however, complicates this. In a remarriage where stepchildren are present, this task becomes even more complicated.

For example, consider Beth and Hal, a couple newly married for the first time. Hal loves classical music and listens to it for about an hour on most evenings. Beth knows this is very important to Hal. Beth likes giving her husband his musical space. Doing so reinforces Beth's self-image of being a good wife.

Now put children in this picture. Can Beth still give Hal his musical hour when household tasks have swelled, and she is weary? Is a good wife someone who allows a husband to do his thing or someone who works with a husband to share the responsibilities of family life? Does Hal's time spent listening to music take priority over time spent with their children?

Let's complicate the scene even further by adding stepchildren. Imagine that this is Beth's second marriage. She has two adolescent children who complain they can't do their homework when classical music fills the house. Now what does it mean to be a good wife, particularly if Hal's response is, "Can't you help your children to understand how important this is to me?" It's one thing to be able to say to a husband, "Your children need you, and I need you to help with them." It's another thing to say, "My children need for you to give them quiet." How can Beth maintain her identity as a good wife and still protect and help her children?

2) What does it mean to be a stepparent? If you are the stepparent, your identity is even more problematic. Most people have some idea about what it means to be a husband or a wife, even though stepchildren complicate the efforts to fulfill those roles in a satisfying way. They even understand something of what it means to be a parent. But what does it mean to be a stepparent?

If you are a parent, you know that this includes such things as rejoicing in, loving, disciplining, and nurturing your children. If you are a stepparent, do you do the same? What if you don't feel love for your stepchild? To what extent do you participate in disciplining your stepchild? How do you nurture someone who has already had years of nurturing before you entered the picture? How do you rejoice in someone who resists your efforts at closeness?

We'll address these questions in other parts of this book. Here, these questions underscore the problematic nature of your identity as a stepparent—problematic partly because there is little consensus on the role of stepparent and partly because stepparenting is typically tolerated rather than preferred.

Research with thirty-two stepfamilies revealed five different stepparenting styles among the families. Some stepfathers tried to act as biological parents. Some stepmothers tried to become "super good" stepmothers. A third style was the "detached" stepparent who had little or no involvement with the stepchildren. Fourth, some stepparents adopted an "uncertain" style; they were essentially at a loss about how to act and stressed by the situation. Fifth, some employed a "friendship" style, attempting to be more of a friend than a parental figure. Clearly, there is no consensus on what it means to be a stepparent.

3) What does it mean to be a child in a stepfamily? Children's identities also can be troublesome in a stepfamily. Jack and Stephanie's first Christmas after their marriage posed a challenge to one of Jack's children. In his first marriage, Jack's children had opened their presents on Christmas morning. But in Stephanie's first marriage, the family had opened presents on Christmas eve. After much discussion, Jack and Stephanie finally decided that the children could open one present each on Christmas eve and the others on Christmas morning after church.

This worked well, with one exception. Jack had forgotten that his first wife had started a tradition of one "special" present for each child—a present that was more expensive than the others and always wrapped in different paper. It was only after looking at his youngest son's sober face for a good part of Christmas day that Jack remembered the tradition.

Fortunately, Jack and Stephanie were sensitive enough to notice his demeanor and astute enough to encourage him to talk about his feelings. What they discovered, in essence, was that he missed the traditional special gift. To him, this gift had always told him he was a special person. He wondered if he was still special. Of course, no one else had gotten a special gift either. Did this mean, he wondered, "Is this to be a family in which no one is special?"

Children's identities are threatened not only by the loss of traditions. The complexities of new situations and relationships also can be threatening. If there is a shared custody arrangement, the children may find themselves continually thrust between two different worlds, with differing rules and contrary patterns of behavior. If children live with stepsiblings, they may feel displaced from their previous positions in their families. They may no longer be the oldest or the youngest child, the only girl or the only boy. Such altered circumstances can be difficult for children.

You will face multiple challenges to your identity in a stepfamily. The challenge, therefore, is for each of you to protect existing elements and nurture new aspects of your identities in positive and constructive ways.

PROTECTING AND NURTURING YOUR IDENTITY

Who am I? Here are some guidelines to help you answer this question:

1) Accept your stepfamily as God's call to a new life. God often calls his children to newness. We label this the Abraham Principle. God called Abraham to leave his country and settle in a new place (Genesis 12). When Abraham was ninety-nine years old, God made a covenant with him and changed his name to Abraham (Genesis 17:1-8). In other words, God kept calling Abraham to newness during his life. Thus, Abraham's identity changed over the course of his walk with God.

Think of the Abraham Principle at work as you join together in a stepfamily. This is God's calling for you. It means each member of the stepfamily needs to be open to change and to becoming the kind of person that God calls each to be. In this way, you can create a family life together, rather than struggle to defend old patterns.

To the stepparent, the Abraham Principle means God has called you not just to your spouse but to your stepchildren as well. Don't view stepchildren as people you have to tolerate in order to remarry, but as an integral part of your calling to newness. To the stepchildren, similarly, the Abraham Principle means that God has called you to relate to your stepparent in a way that will be beneficial to all of you.

At the beginning of your regular family meetings (see chapter 2), or as part of a weekly devotional time, we suggest you read the following affirmation:

> God has led us into a new family. It will not be like our old families, but it will be good because God has brought us together. We thank him for the opportunity to love, support, understand, and encourage each other. And we pray that, by his grace, we will live together and relate to one another in a way which provides each of us with the abundant life he wills for us.

Help each member of your stepfamily to think of your life together not in terms of struggle on a purely human plane, but in terms of a response to God's call to newness. This doesn't mean there not will be any struggles. Rather, it means you can see those struggles in a different light—as efforts to live out the new life to which God has called you and as part of the work of fashioning new identities that are in accord with God's will.

2) Retain as much of the old as is reasonable and mutually desirable. The Abraham Principle doesn't mean total transformation. God never told Abraham to abandon all of his traditions and habits when he moved to a new land or when he accepted his new name. Those valued traditions, habits, and patterns of living that are not inconsistent with, or disruptive to, the new stepfamily should be retained.

Thus, we noted that Jack and Stephanie had contrary styles of handling disagreements. Because neither Stephanie nor her children were comfortable with Jack's style of loud confrontation, he agreed to modify the way he argued. This meant a change in his identity because his style was to meet conflict head-on and push for a quick resolution.

However, the new approach was beneficial to him. As Jack nurtured this new aspect of his identity, he discovered that it enriched, rather than deprived, him. He now sees himself as someone who is flexible in handling disagreements. He is no longer boxed in by a single style that may not be appropriate for every situation. Instead, he can adapt his style in keeping with his expanded set of interpersonal skills.

On another issue, Jack and Stephanie decided that he should continue to display affection openly. This was a valued part of his identity. Unlike many men he knew, Jack could express his feelings both verbally and nonverbally without embarrassment. However, they agreed they needed to discuss the matter with the children. As it turned out, Stephanie was correct in her belief that Jack's children resented his open displays of affection for her. They are helping the children to understand that Jack's affection for Stephanie does not detract from their mother as a person. Rather, they explained to Jack's children that the expression of affection is important in creating a strong bond in their new marriage. And strengthening this bond added stability and security to their stepfamily.

Jack and Stephanie also agreed not to demand radical changes in the children's way of doing things around the house. For example, Jack's children had always been allowed to have snacks in the family room while watching TV. Initially, Stephanie was appalled by the idea because she thought the house would be messy. However, she talked the matter over with Jack and wisely decided to allow them to continue the practice with the condition that they clean up after themselves. We say "wisely" because her accommodation was a small price to pay for maintaining a privilege valued by her stepchildren. Had she insisted that the practice stop, furthermore, she would have given her stepchildren a new message about their identity: "You are messy. And I care more about the house than I do about you."

Of course, eating a snack in the family room may seem like a trivial matter. But for children, permission to continue habitual ways of behaving can be of enormous value in helping them feel secure. It means that at least some part of the world they have known is still the same, that their lives have not been totally turned inside out.

3) Look on the new as an adventure in growth. At first, Jack wasn't pleased at the prospect of changing his style of handling conflict. Eventually, however, he realized that it was a growth experience for him. His new way of handling conflict made him feel better about himself in several ways. He felt more adept at handling conflict. His new approach was calmer and less explosive. As a result, the family could focus on solving the problem rather than hiding from Jack's anger when conflict occurred. Moreover, the change in Jack was very pleasing to Stephanie and thereby enhanced their intimacy.

Newness includes a variety of things, of course, ranging from new menus at mealtime to new ways of handling household chores to new leisure activities. Whatever the new thing may be, someone in the stepfamily may not be sold on it and may vigorously resist it. For example, Sue, a stepmother of two boys—ages 8 and 11—loves cooking ethnic foods. Her husband, Brad, is intrigued and enthusiastic about her culinary creations. But her stepsons complained that these different foods were "weird," "yucky," and "not what our mom makes for us." Needless to say, their dinner table had become a war zone.

Sue and Brad tried several approaches to solving the problem. For a time, they insisted the children eat whatever Sue prepared, but this approach turned into a nightmare and escalated the war. Then, Sue began to fix separate dishes for the children; but she resented the time and expense this required. Finally, Sue, Brad, and the children came up with a plan together. First, Sue would do most of her experimental cooking during the week when the boys stayed with their mother. Second, the boys would help Sue plan the weekend menus which featured their favorite foods. Finally, on one Saturday every month, they would have an ethnic dinner. It was to be a family effort: they would decide together which region or nation to celebrate; Sue would plan the menu; Brad and the boys would decorate the dinner table and help Sue with the cooking and cleanup. Sue says this plan has worked well for her stepfamily. "We've all gotten something out of it that we wanted and, more importantly, our monthly ethnic events have bonded us together as a family."

4) Understand why family members may initially resist change. If you think Sue and Brad's solution is an unworkable solution because people "just won't change," we have good news for you. Contrary to the popular idea that everyone resists the new, people only resist change under certain circumstances. In particular, we all tend to resist change when we perceive that change to be:

• a threat of some kind. It may be a financial threat, a threat to our self-esteem, a threat to our status, a threat to a valued relationship, and so on. No one likes to be threatened.

• imposed on us. God made us as creatures who have choice, and thus, we resist when our free will is supplanted by someone else's choice.

• too vague in terms of its consequences. "What will this change mean for me?" is a question that immediately comes to most of us. If there is no clear answer, we are likely to resist.

• too costly. The cost may be anything from inconvenience to a sustained effort to change a habit. If the benefits are not greater than the cost, we will resist.

What we hope is clear from the above is the need to understand why a family member resists doing something in a new way. You need to address the concerns (another good reason for family meetings), then help the resistor define the change as an adventure in growth (unless, of course, the resistor convinces the rest of you that a particular new way really is a threat rather than an opportunity for growth).

5) Take steps to minimize confusion and strain. Times of confusion and strain can threaten identity. When you are living in the midst of great ambiguity and uncertainty, it is difficult to maintain a firm sense of who you are. Thus, you protect your identity when you minimize ambiguity and instability as much as possible.

Note that we say "minimize." You can't eliminate confusion and strain altogether, but you can minimize them. Consider again the case of Jack and Stephanie. Their relationship was severely strained because they differed over the appropriate way to celebrate their children's birthdays. The first birthday they confronted after their marriage was that of Jack's daughter. When Stephanie talked about the party she planned and the presents she intended to buy, Jack was dumbfounded. It was simply too much. If Stephanie insisted, then he insisted that a part of the presents would be from him and the others would be from Stephanie. However, they realized that could create confusion. Jack's daughter would wonder why she received separate presents. Furthermore, Jack and Stephanie knew the children would sense their disagreement about the matter.

They worked out a compromise—one that provided a less elaborate celebration than Stephanie wanted but cost more than Jack preferred. They agreed to limit both the number of friends the children could invite to their birthday parties (no more than ten) and the number of gifts Jack and Stephanie bought for them (no more than three).

Feelings of uncertainty and stress can be particularly intense in homes where one spouse's children reside permanently and the other spouse's children visit on a regular basis. The children who visit are particularly likely to feel the strain of being in a strange place, of being "away from home." If possible, the visiting children should have their own room and beds. If this isn't possible, they should have something (a closet, a desk, or other personal items) that connects them to their stepfamily and tells them this is also their home. In addition, visiting children need to understand and abide by the rules of the house. These may differ from the rules at their other home but, nevertheless, they apply. It's not a matter of "when you come here, you have to . . . ," but "in this house we all . . ."

A calendar, which enables them to keep track of their schedules, is also helpful in reducing uncertainty among children who spend time in two separate homes. A calendar entitled "My Two Homes" is currently on the market. It includes stickers for children to indicate which days they are with which parent, which days they switch homes, which days they have music lessons or dental appointments, and so on. Whether you purchase such a calendar or make your own, giving the children a visual reminder will ease the confusion and strain of their complicated schedules.

6) Encourage every family member to grow. A fair amount of stepfamily life involves damage control—efforts to deal with past hurts and present struggles. In the process, it is easy to forget one of the more valuable things stepfamily members can do for each other—encourage each other's growth. When you encourage each other's growth, you are protecting and nurturing each other's identities.

To encourage growth is to affirm and celebrate the individuality of each member of the stepfamily. This probably won't come naturally or easily. For instance, you place a high priority on getting along together. And you may think that getting along means family members should share the same ideas and opinions. But thinking alike is an unreasonable goal—one more likely to produce boredom rather than harmony.

Thus, Jack and Stephanie haven't tried to mute their political differences. Their differences make for lively table conversation at times and provide an excellent civics lesson. Moreover, the children can observe the incredible model of two people who differ strongly on some issues, but who continue to love each other passionately. Jack and Stephanie are teaching their children to be individuals in their thinking. They are also teaching them to respect differences.

You encourage growth when you expose family members to diverse ideas and respect their conclusions about those ideas. Similarly, parents encourage growth when they permit children to make some of their own decisions. A stepchild may want to arrange his or her room in a way that you dislike or wear clothes that you find tasteless. As long as you and your spouse agree that the child doesn't look ludicrous or the room isn't offensive, let the child decide.

Finally, you can encourage growth by noting and supporting special talents and interests. A man whose home is decorated with some of his own artwork told us:

> "I never thought of myself as an artist when I was young. I remember drawing illustrations when I was in elementary school. My teacher thought they were great and hung them on the classroom wall for a few weeks. But when I took my drawings home, neither my mother nor my stepfather had much to say. I guess in their eyes, I was not artistic. It wasn't until I was an adult that I had the urge to try art again."

This man's family missed an opportunity to encourage his growth. In fact, his stepfather missed many opportunities. The man is clearly competent, but he told us, "The only thing I recall my step-father encouraging me to do was to follow him and go into the oil business. But I have no interest or talent for that kind of work."

We believe that every individual has creative potential. Some people may be creative in the arts, in the sciences, in interpersonal relations, or in mechanical skills. We urge you, therefore, to look for the creative potential in your children, in your stepchildren, and in each other. Affirm, support, and encourage the development of this creative potential. In doing so, you are nurturing and protecting each other's identities.

7) Protect your self-esteem. It is also important for you to nurture and protect your own identity. In particular, you need to protect your self-esteem. Even without being in a stepfamily, your self-esteem can be impacted by many things: failures, criticism, inability to reach a goal, or alienation from a former friend.

The failure of marriage is an assault on most people's self-esteem. Remarriage is a reaffirmation of self-esteem. But living in a stepfamily can be another assault, particularly when the stresses of stepfamily life cause the marriage to founder. At such times, you need a healthy dose of self-esteem in order to muster the energy and hope necessary to deal with the stressful times.

If each of you is following our sixth suggestion and encouraging each other to grow, you already have one source of protection for your self-esteem. It is especially important for husband and wife to not only encourage growth, but also to support each other. In addition, express your appreciation. Let your spouse know how much you value his or her contributions to the quality of your family life.

One of the more common assaults on self-esteem is the rejection that stepparents experience from stepchildren. The rejection may be chronic or occasional. It can also take a variety of forms: hostility, indifference, coldness, refusal to cooperate, or passive-aggressive behavior, which means to behave in a way that appears to be cooperative but that is actually subversive. Even young children can be passive-aggressive.

For example, you tell your stepchild that he could really help you out by picking up his room. He agrees to do this, but it never happens. You tell him again, and he seems contrite and agrees to help. It still doesn't happen. What you may be facing is not a child who is irresponsible but rather passive-aggressive behavior which is a sign of his rejection.

Rejection hurts. Moreover, it can damage your self-esteem if you interpret the rejection to mean that you are not good enough, or not persistent enough, or not attractive enough to win your stepchild's acceptance.

There are a number of steps you can take to handle rejection and to protect your self-esteem. First, be honest about how you feel. Don't pretend the rejection doesn't hurt when it does. Occasionally, a stepparent will try to deny the rejection and work all the harder to somehow please a stepchild. However, there are limits to how long you can deny your feelings. So acknowledge your hurt from the beginning, before it erupts into rage.

Second, enlist the aid of your spouse. Be honest with your spouse as well as with yourself. You need your spouse's reassurance that you are a lovable, caring person in spite of the rejection.

Third, keep the rejection in perspective. Remind yourself of the people who appreciate you. Remind yourself of the effective interpersonal skills you have demonstrated in other situations. In other words, keep in mind that it is your stepchild who has rejected you, not the world. Also keep in mind that stepchildren are quite adept at rejecting.

Fourth, focus on what you are doing that is right. An understandable reaction to rejection is asking, "What am I doing that's wrong?" Of course, you may have made some mistakes. Who doesn't? Parents make mistakes with their own children as well as with stepchildren. However, once you correct any mistakes, focus on what you're doing that is right. You might, for instance, say to yourself, "I am trying to be a good stepparent. I encourage and support my stepchild. It's okay for me to get distressed and hurt when he (she) doesn't appreciate this. I'll recover, and I'll continue to be a good stepparent."

Remind yourself of the enormity of God's love for you. We once heard a sermon in which the pastor elaborated on the meaning of Jesus' words, "I do not call you servants any longer . . . but I have called you friends" (John 15:15). Among other things, the pastor said to keep in mind what it means when you call someone a friend. You are saying to that person, "I regard you as someone special in my life; I treasure you." Similarly, in calling us friends, Jesus is telling us that he regards us each as very special, as someone he treasures.

When you start to feel like a failure, when your self-esteem starts dropping around your ankles, remind yourself that you are a very special person to God. God treasures you. So renew your efforts to build your stepfamily, not in the spirit of one who is incapable or incompetent or unlovable, but in the spirit of one who is treasured and sustained by God.

Who Are We?

The Challenge of Family Identity

We once asked a class of college students to write a paper describing their family relationships. We wanted to see to what extent they were involved with their extended family—grandparents, uncles and aunts, cousins, and so forth. One young woman brought an enormous posterboard to class. She explained that the relationships were so complex, she couldn't describe them in mere words. She was part of a stepfamily, which was intricate in itself because she was involved with eight grandparents and numerous other relatives and step-relatives. But her situation was further complicated by the fact that one of her uncles had divorced his wife and married one of the student's step-aunts. And he had children from both marriages. Even with the help of the chart, we were left in a confused state.

Hopefully, your extended family is not as complicated as this student's. But all stepfamilies are complex and, therefore, pose a practical and an emotional challenge. The sheer size of the family can be initially overwhelming. Think of all those with whom you may have to relate: your former spouse and parent of your children; your children's grandparents, aunts, uncles, and cousins; plus your step-children's grandparents, aunts, uncles, and cousins. The list goes on and on. The practical task of maintaining connections and sharing family experiences, such as holidays, with even the most important of these family members is a daunting one.

Moreover, there is the challenge of what to call these relatives. What should a stepdaughter call her stepfather when she calls her own father "Dad"? This is a practical as well as a very emotional concern. Or how do you refer to your ex-mother-in-law whom you have always called "Mom" when you now have a new mother-in-law with whom you don't feel nearly as comfortable? Or what should your son call his stepsister's grandparents?

These are some of the challenges we will examine in this chapter. They all bear upon the issue of family identity, which is as important to your well-being as your personal identity.

WHAT IS FAMILY IDENTITY?

When you ask, "Who am I?" you raise the question of personal identity. When you ask, "Who are we?" you raise the question of family identity. In other words, just as your personal identity is your sense of who you are and of what makes you distinct from other people, your family identity is your sense of who belongs in your family and what makes your family distinct from others. Let's look at these two elements of family identity.

1) Who belongs in your family? This question is important because family members are expected to treat each other in ways that may not apply to nonfamily members (such as observing birthdays, lending financial help, and giving support during times of difficulty). Family members have a special bond with each other. Family members have obligations to each other that they may not feel toward outsiders. Robert Frost captured this idea in his poem, "The Death of the Hired Man," when he wrote:

> "Home is the place where, when you have to go there,
> They have to take you in."

In addition, some family members are more central than others in terms of your bonds and your obligations. Generally, you feel closer to, and more responsible for, your parents than your aunts and uncles, your children than your nieces and nephews, your siblings than your cousins, and so forth.

The question of who belongs in the family is not as simple as it may appear. What about uncle Sam's alcoholic wife? Is she really a member of the family, a member in the sense we have just described? What about dad's mother, who abandoned the family to pursue her career? What about your cousin's children, who are virtual strangers to you? Do you feel any bonds with them or any obligations toward them?

When you think about the large group of people who could technically—by blood or marriage—be called a part of your family, they fall into different categories. Some are clearly a part of your family; you feel a special bond with them. Others are marginal. And some may not be included when you identify who is really part of your family.

2) What makes your family distinct? An important part of family identity is the sense that "this is the kind of people we are." Early on, children learn what makes their family distinct. They learn by explicit instruction. For example, every time a parent says to a child, "We don't do that," the parent is building family identity. They learn by rituals and traditions: "We are the kind of people who worship regularly. We are the kind of people who regard birthdays as times of special celebration. We are the kind of people who talk about the events of the day at the dinner table." And they learn by modeling— by observing the way that various family members think and behave.

Of course, when we say that your family identity is distinct, we do not mean that it differs from every other family in every way. Other families worship regularly, treat birthdays in a special way, and discuss the day's events at the dinner table. But only your family has the total package—the particular people, rituals, traditions, and practices—that comprise your family identity.

Because family identity is one way of saying "this is the kind of people we are," it is a significant part of your personal identity.

When you were a child, your family identity was a significant factor in giving form to your personal identity. As you grew, various other factors affected your personal identity. Your developing personal identity, in turn, may have modified your family identity. When you married and began a new family, both your's and your spouse's personal identities helped give form to a new family identity.

Thus, there is an ongoing exchange between family and personal identities. Each influences the other, and each is essential to your well-being. We saw in the last chapter how stepfamily life complicates personal identities. Now let's think about how it also complicates family identity.

THE COMPLEXITIES OF STEPFAMILY IDENTITY

Sorting out who belongs, what we're about, and for whom we are responsible is a complex and demanding task for any family; it's even more so for a stepfamily. Yet it's a necessary task, at the very least, for your emotional and physical well-being. (You could go berserk trying to keep up with the overwhelming number of family commitments in a stepfamily.) And it's also necessary task if your goal is to forge a successful stepfamily.

Even in a biological family, your obligations certainly vary depending upon the nature of the relationship. As we noted above, you typically would not feel the same responsibility for a cousin as for a sibling or a parent or a child. But again, in a stepfamily, the question of responsibilities becomes more complex. Do you have the same obligations to your spouse's children as to your own? Do you have the same obligation to your spouse's children if they only live part time in your home as you do if they live there all the time? Are children for whom there is shared custody always considered part of the family when plans or decisions are made—even when those children are not present? Or do they slip in and out of family consideration as they move back and forth between homes?

Circumstances can change, even after you have decided such matters. Fred and Terry each brought children to their marriage, and each had a shared custody arrangement with their ex-spouse. Fred had one daughter, and Terry had a daughter and a son. For a few years, the shared custody arrangements worked well; in fact, Fred and Terry even managed a certain amount of time at home without any children. They thought of themselves as a fluid family in which they had only partial responsibility for the three children. Their ex-spouses assumed the remaining responsibility.

But Terry's ex-spouse had remarried and her daughter had increasing difficulties with her new stepmother. After a few years, it was agreed that she would live full time with Fred and Terry. Quickly their family identity changed and became problematic. Terry's ex-husband still wanted to have major input in his daughter's life. Suddenly he and his wife became a part of Fred and Terry's family. In the past, each couple had celebrated special occasions in the daughter's life separately. Each couple also had equal, but separate, involvement in her education, health care, and extracurricular activities. She had separate sets of clothes at each house. In other words, there was minimal contact between the two couples. However, once the daughter lived in one home, the couples had to have more contact. Both family identities changed. And both changed in a way that neither family preferred.

Similarly, when Peter married Joan, he became a stepfather to Joan's daughter. Joan and her ex-husband have joint custody. Peter tells about some of the difficulties they have experienced in establishing a family identity:

> "When I married Joan, I definitely felt like an outsider whenever a problem arose with her daughter. In a number of arguments, it was them against me. I recall times when I had to leave the room or even the house in order to cool off and try to get the thing into perspective.
>
> "Joan and I have had two children. So now it's my stepdaughter who feels like an outsider. She says she prefers to stay with her father because she's an only child there. She gets all of her father's attention. Joan and I have been working hard to let her know that we consider her a very important part of our fam-

ily as well. But she still spends more time with her father than she does with us. And this really hurts Joan."

Peter and Joan have worked hard to create a strong sense of family identity, but they have not found it an easy task. They, like Fred and Terry, are attempting to build a solid family on the remains of former family ties and traditions. It's a demanding and complex task, but it's also a necessary one. If you want a successful stepfamily, you must develop a reliable family identity. You must be able to think of your stepfamily in terms of "this is the kind of people we are."

THE IMPERATIVE OF STEPFAMILY IDENTITY

By this point, it should be clear that to establish your identity as a stepfamily, each member must agree on who is part of your family and what kind of people you are. To achieve this, you need to answer a whole series of vexing questions: "Who are all these people?"; "What do I call them?"; "How do I relate to them?"; "How do they fit into the way our family functions?"; "What does it mean to me to be part of this family?" If you don't have the answers to these questions, it will be difficult to relate to your family members in a meaningful and harmonious way. Rather, your interactions will be awkward at best, and conflicted or alienated at worst.

For example, consider the question of what stepchildren should call their stepparents. When given a choice, most stepchildren choose to call stepparents by their first names or by special nicknames. "Mom" and "Dad" are usually reserved for biological parents, and this helps a child clarify his or her personal identity. No matter how close the relationship is with the stepparent, it is important for a child to know something about both biological parents. A woman who grew up with a stepmother whom she always called "mom" told us of her reaction when she became a young adult:

"My mother died shortly after I was born. I never knew her. My earliest memories of a mother are of my stepmother. She has always been my mom, and always will be. When I was a young girl, I learned that she was my stepmother. This didn't bother me at the time. As far as I was concerned, she was a great mother.

"Then, shortly after my 20th birthday, my attention was captured by a mother and her baby who were sitting across from me on the subway. You could tell the mother adored her baby. Watching them, I felt this strong urge to know the woman who had given birth to me. I wasn't rejecting my stepmother, but my father had told me very little about my real mother. And I felt that both my mother and I had been cheated because I knew almost nothing about her. Besides, I carry her genes. Even though I never knew her, she's part of me."

In this case, we don't quarrel with the decision to call the stepmother "Mom" from the beginning. An infant needs a mom, not a "Jane." Yet the father was so anxious to replicate a biological family, so anxious for her to think of her stepmother as her mother, that he erred by not telling his daughter about her mother.

In some cases, a child may eventually choose to call a stepparent "Mom" or "Dad." A stepfather told us that one of the high points of his life was when his stepdaughter came to him and said, "Would it be all right if I started calling you Dad instead of Jimmy?"

In establishing a stepfamily identity, relationships with grandparents often pose a particularly difficult challenge. The challenges include: struggles between grandparents and former daughters- or sons-in-law; fears of losing contact with grandchildren; the sudden inheritance of a ready-made stepgrandchild; and fair treatment in families with both biological and stepgrandchildren.

As stepparents, you need to be clear and reasonable about your obligations to grandparents. It is difficult enough, particularly on holidays, for parents to juggle what they feel are their obligations to their children and two sets of grandparents. But if three or four sets of grandparents are involved, the juggling act can be harrowing for you as well as your children—even when they are older. Veronica is a young woman who grew up splitting her time between her mother's and father's homes. Both parents were remarried. She tells of the agony she endured when she was a college student:

"I would come home for holidays, and my father would want me to visit with his family and my stepmother's family. My mother, of course, wanted the same for her and my stepfather's family. I just didn't have the time or energy to do everything they wanted me to do.

"My father usually would become very angry with me because he holds family gatherings as sacred. Once, he accused me of neglecting my family responsibilities. He even said that I had apparently chosen not to be a part of his family. I got to the point that I just dreaded any holiday."

CREATING A STEPFAMILY IDENTITY

Creating a clear stepfamily identity won't solve all your problems, but the failure to create one will greatly add to the problems you face. Among the things you can do to establish your own stepfamily identity are the following:

1) Establish priorities. Establishing priorities means to decide which among those related to you through blood or marriage will be central, which of them will be marginal, and which will not be included in your stepfamily activities. This may sound cold and calculating, but time and energy limitations prevent you from including everyone. As the case of Veronica illustrates, you may not be able to meet all of the expectations or wishes of family members.

Who gets first claim on your time and energy? (Keep in mind that crises or other unusual situations can temporarily alter your priorities.) Your nuclear stepfamily, including any shared custody arrangements, will have first priority. Beyond this, however, priorities can vary from one stepfamily to another. The important thing is to have them.

How do you establish your relational priorities? Begin by discussing such questions as:

• What obligations do we have for important events—like birthdays, graduations, and weddings—in the lives of various relatives?

• With whom will we observe holidays?

• What responsibilities do we have for visiting relatives or for entertaining relatives in our home?

• What financial obligations, if any, do we have for children not living in our home or for parents or other relatives?

• In case of schedule conflicts or time limitations, what kind of activity generally has priority—school, family, religious, recreational, or personal development (such as music lessons or participation in sports)?

The point of discussing such questions is not to draw up a rigid list of commitments. Rather, it is to provide general guidelines so you won't have to deal with every situation on a spontaneous (and perhaps anguished) basis. The recurring problem between Veronica and her father could have been avoided if her father had talked about family responsibilities with her, rather than assuming that she owed as much to her stepmother's family as she did to her mother's.

Incidentally, Veronica's situation illustrates an important point about priorities—they can differ among stepfamily members. Her father and stepmother placed great importance on going to a birthday party for Veronica's stepgrandmother. Veronica chose to use the occasion to visit her mother's parents. Such differing priorities can be practical ways to deal with the complexities of stepfamily life—unless, like Veronica's father, you try to enforce the same priorities on every family member.

2) Balance stepfamily priorities with personal preferences.
Stepfamily members can have different priorities, but individual preferences cannot always be fulfilled. There needs to be an ongoing effort to balance stepfamily priorities and personal preferences. There are some things for which individual preferences should be followed. We suggested earlier that mature children should be allowed to choose their own names for stepfamily relations. You can offer them a variety of choices, but the selection should be theirs.

When personal preferences are less important than stepfamily priorities, this situation is ripe for conflict and struggle. We recommend that you keep in mind a principle we discussed in chapter 3: distinguish between problems unique to the stepfamily and those that would have occurred in any case. Every family has to deal with times when personal preferences clash with a family priority. So don't automatically assume that each time you clash it is because you are a stepfamily; that turns the clash into another mark against stepfamily life when it may simply reflect a struggle that could happen in any family.

For example, Rex and Faith had an argument because her nine-year-old son did not want to go to the home of Rex's parents for Christmas brunch. "We talked about it," Rex pointed out, "and agreed from the start that we would go to the brunch because it was a tradition in our family." Faith admitted she had agreed to go but backed down when she realized how strongly her son objected. Rex accused her of going back on her word. Faith accused him of being inflexible and insensitive to her son.

Both Rex and Faith overlooked something important. At his age, her son would probably not have wanted to go anywhere after just opening all his Christmas presents. The fact that it was the home of his stepfather's parents was irrelevant. Faith, however, immediately assumed this was a stepfamily problem and was distressed. Her son quickly picked up on Faith's distress and objected even more dramatically—hoping that his mother would take his side against his stepfather.

In other words, the boy would have objected to going anywhere. He may not have objected as strongly, however, if he had not noted how quickly his mother took his side. She missed an opportunity to teach her son that individual preferences sometimes give way to stepfamily priorities. He probably would have still objected, of course. He may have sulked and complained as they drove to Rex's parent's home. But Rex and Faith would have avoided an argument and the son would have learned something important about living in a stepfamily.

3) *Accept your limitations.* In essence, this means to accept the fact that some otherwise good things won't get done as you follow your priorities. When a man came up to Jesus and offered to follow him after first burying his father, Jesus replied, "Follow me, and let the dead bury their own dead" (Matthew 8:22).

Biblical commentators have pointed out that the man's offer was probably not about the immediate burial of his father who had just died. Rather, the man was saying that some day after his father died he would follow Jesus. Obviously, it is a good thing to spend time with your father. In rejecting the man's request, Jesus implied that when you have priorities in life, some things that are good in themselves may be left undone.

This is the point that Veronica made to her father when they came to us for help. She was not rejecting her stepmother or her stepmother's family. She agreed it would be a good thing to spend some time with her stepmother's family—a way of reinforcing her solidarity with the stepfamily. "But," she pointed out, "there just isn't time." To spend time with her stepmother's family meant not spending time with her mother's parents (with whom she was very close). Hopefully, Veronica's father now understands that, in choosing to give her mother's family priority over her stepmother's, Veronica is living with her human limitations. She is not declaring her stepmother's family unimportant. She is simply saying that some otherwise good things can't be done in the face of so many responsibilities and needs.

4) *Maintain flexibility.* Let's say you have established your priorities and set up a workable balance between individual preferences and stepfamily priorities. No need to be concerned about those issues any more, right? Not necessarily. Those who have a satisfying stepfamily life point out that flexibility is even more important in stepfamilies than in biological families. As one stepparent put it:

> "In my first marriage, my husband and I made plans for holidays, vacations, and leisure activities, and that was that. Once we set them up, we didn't have to change them. But when you're in

a stepfamily, you have to be willing to change your plans—even at the last minute, like the time my husband and I were going on a trip by ourselves so we could focus on each other. My kids were scheduled to spend the week with their father. And he cancelled two days before we were to leave because of something he had to do with his wife's family."

So one aspect of flexibility is a willingness (even if it is a disgruntled willingness) to alter your plans when necessary. A second aspect is the willingness to accommodate differing traditions into your stepfamily identity. One way to do this is to change one tradition in order to maintain another. Rex and Faith, for example, could have changed their traditional Christmas morning present exchange with a Christmas Eve exchange. This would have given Faith's son more time with his presents and still maintained the tradition of brunch at Rex's parents' home. Or they could have started a new tradition and invited Rex's family to their home for Christmas brunch.

Another way to accommodate differing traditions is to expend the extra time and energy to fulfill them when possible. We know of a mother who spends hours taking her daughter to her father's home on Christmas so the child can continue to spend at least a part of the holiday with both biological parents. We know of a stepfamily where the children have two Christmas celebrations— one on December 25 and one on December 26 so that each biological parent can celebrate with the child.

Frankly, such arrangements sound exhausting to us. But they do display a remarkable amount of flexibility on the part of the couples, each of whom is striving to build a satisfying stepfamily life. In each case, the parents would personally prefer to celebrate in different ways but know that their flexibility is beneficial to their children. It not only allows the children special time with their biological parents, it also shows them that they are part of a family that can adapt to differing, unexpected, and even contrary demands. This is a positive attribute of their family identity that they can incorporate into their personal identities.

5) *Be gentle and patient as you cultivate solidarity.* To have a family identity means to have a sense of "we-ness." It means solidarity. And remember that solidarity does not mean the absence of conflict and total agreement on every issue. In a vain effort to create instant solidarity, stepparents often try to maintain complete harmony or try to make everyone be carbon copies of each other. Some cases in point:

• the family that tries to squelch all disagreements and all arguing.

• the mother who insists that her children kiss their stepfather goodnight before going to bed, even though they were reluctant to do so.

• the family that insists that every member believe the same thing about issues such as dating, politics, and even which sports teams to support.

• the father who wants his daughter to say that her stepmother was more of a "real" mother to her than was her biological mother.

• the mother who insists that her adolescent son spend time with his stepgrandmother as a way of letting her know that he was as much a part of the stepfamily as he was of his biological family.

These efforts are well-intentioned but counterproductive ways to develop solidarity. Solidarity as a stepfamily cannot be forced. It must be patiently cultivated rather than quickly created.

The need for patience was underscored by a stepfather who has a very satisfying stepfamily. His stepdaughter spends half her time with him and his wife, and the other half with her father. Today, he introduces her to strangers as his daughter, and she likes this. They have a solid stepfamily, but it was not always so. We asked him how it came about, and what he would recommend to other stepparents who are trying to build solidarity:

"Be a listener. Don't be discouraged if you're ignored by your stepchild. It takes a lot of time for the stepchild to come around. You have to let him respond on his own time schedule and not on yours. Always be available to him but don't force it. On the other hand, you shouldn't be a patsy and let your stepchild walk over you. If your stepchild is clearly out of line, treat your stepchild just like you would your own children. Also let him know how you feel about his behavior."

You can summarize what this successful stepfather said with a principle: build solidarity by proceeding at the stepchild's pace and by following the stepparent's rules. The rules include points we have made previously: don't pretend everything is okay if it isn't; confront problems directly but not harshly; and don't try to force a stepchild into an intimacy for which he or she isn't ready.

6) Be gentle and patient as you help stepsiblings relate to each other. Family solidarity includes good relationships between stepsiblings. In helping them relate well to each other, keep in mind that many stepfamily problems are encountered in biological families as well. Take sibling rivalry, for example. Don't assume that stepsibling rivalry is a sign that your stepfamily is not working well. It may be just a sign that your children are developing normally.

To some extent, you can let stepsiblings work out their own problems. When they work through rivalries and jealousies on their own, they develop useful interpersonal skills and are more likely to wind up as friends. At other times, however, they are likely to need your help. Remember to be gentle and patient. You need to be gentle because, as in the case of stepparent-stepchild relationships, you can't enforce intimacy and harmony. You need to be patient because good stepsibling relationships are not likely to develop as quickly as you would like them to; again, they have to develop at the children's pace.

An important way to help children is to encourage them to be open and honest about their feelings. Among other things, this means you never say to a child, "You shouldn't feel that way." At the very least, this will discourage the child from sharing any feelings in the future. A better approach, even in cases of statements or hatred, is to encourage the child to talk about the behavior of the stepsibling that contributes to the feeling.

For instance, assume that Johnny and his stepbrother, Kevin, are constantly bickering. Johnny's mother wants to end their quarreling and help them become more compatible. This could be her conversation with Johnny:

> M: "Johnny, you and Kevin seem to be having a tough time getting along with each other. What's the problem?"
> J: "I hate him. I don't want him here."
> M [resisting the impulse to say "I wish you didn't feel that way"]: "What is it about him that you hate?"
> J: "He always takes my toys without asking. He acts like they're his."
> M: "I can see why this would make you angry. Why don't we talk with him and see if we can work this out."

We are not suggesting that all stepsibling problems can be resolved as easily as the one above. But notice what is going on. The mother lets Johnny know that his feelings are understandable and that it is helpful to talk about them. She also shows him that something can be done to change the situation that has generated his negative feelings. This is a problem-solving approach. It requires more patience than other approaches, but it is also far more effective.

In addition, encourage your child to talk about the whole step-family situation; "hatred" of a stepsibling may be rooted more in his or her anxieties about loss of your love than it is in anything the stepsibling has done. It's possible that Johnny's hatred of Kevin reflects his anxiety that Kevin's father is alienating Johnny's mother from him.

Consequently, another important way to help stepsiblings relate well with each other is to make each child feel equally loved and valued. This helps in two ways. It makes the child feel secure and able to relate better to others, including his or her stepsiblings. It also forces the child to see stepsiblings in a new light, as someone loved and valued by their parent. The likely result is that improved stepsibling relationships will develop.

7) Enlist the aid of grandparents. Sometimes grandparents have a difficult time accepting stepgrandchildren or treating them in the same way they treat their biological grandchildren. So you may need to provide some guidance.

Fred and Terry, whom you met earlier in this chapter, faced these problems with Terry's parents. They often invited Fred and Terry to their home for dinner. However, whenever Terry reminded them that Fred's daughter was staying with them at the time, they would say, "Well, why don't we just wait until another time." Her parents loved Terry's children, but they had never accepted Fred's daughter as a member of their family.

Grandparents can have a crucial role in the success of a stepfamily. They contribute to that success when they do such things as:

• treat all the children equally in such things as gift-giving, invitations, and attending performances and celebrations.

• take a gentle, patient approach to building intimacy with stepgrandchildren, which includes letting the children decide what to call their stepgrandparents.

• treat the new daughter-in-law or son-in-law with the same love and respect as they did the first one.

• celebrate and enjoy the new stepfamily rather than lament the family that broke up.

8) Carefully plan for holidays. As we have noted, a stepfamily often brings together people with differing traditions for observing holidays. Because such observances are a central part of your family identity, you need to plan for them carefully so as to minimize hurts, conflicts, and disappointments.

Part of the planning may involve reminding yourself of your priorities. At times such as Christmas, many biological families are exhausted by the rounds of shopping, programs, parties, and exchanging of gifts. To try to do a double set can, as a stepfather put it, be a "nightmare of chaos."

At such times, you need to stick firmly to the priorities you have set. You may have to cut down on the number of invitations you extend and accept from extended family members. You may have to set limits on the number of, and the amount you spend on, gifts. It is perfectly appropriate to tell people, "We are not going to be able to give as many gifts this year because we have many more people we need to remember."

You will also need to be flexible and creative as you plan. If you bring people together who still find it difficult to relate harmoniously, you may want to gather in a more public place such as a restaurant, a church hall, or a park.

The bottom line is, holidays provide opportunities for memorable family events. Planning effectively helps ensure that your children and stepchildren will have fond memories to carry into adulthood.

9) Build your own stepfamily traditions. Traditions are a central part of family identity. Traditions include the way you celebrate holidays, the rituals you follow (saying grace before meals, discussing the day's activities at dinner, stories at bedtime, etc.), and the way you observe various life benchmarks such as birthdays, graduations, and funerals.

Traditions link you to each other as well as to past and future generations. Traditions can have healing value. For example, we noted in chapter 2 that one way to deal with loss is to have a family meeting; you can extend this and have regular family meetings where each person has the opportunity to discuss his or her current struggles (some of which may be outside the stepfamily itself). Such a tradition can have a healing effect as you strive to understand and support each other.

While you will want to continue some traditions that members bring into the stepfamily, it's important that you build new ones as well. Here are a few activities that other stepfamilies have used to build their special traditions:

- celebrate half-birthdays (the six-month point) as well as regular birthdays.

- have special breakfasts together, with a menu requested by the children, on Saturday or Sunday mornings.

- create a stepfamily album or scrapbook that records special or memorable events.

- have a monthly outing that is chosen alternately by various members of the stepfamily.

- plan to spend a holiday—anything from Halloween to Memorial Day—in a way that no family member has ever before experienced.

- have a regular family activity in which everyone participates (riding bicycles, hiking, playing music, playing games, etc.).

- have a time in the evening when each member of the family shares something good that happened during the day. Then, give God thanks for each other and for each good thing that happened.

Perhaps you can use some of the above ideas in your stepfamily. Or perhaps they can stimulate you to think of other things you might do. In any case, cherish the old traditions you continue to follow; they provide a sense of stability and continuity. Create some new traditions; they build your stepfamily identity and help develop solidarity.

"If I Love You, Do I Stop Loving Him?"

The Challenge of Loyalty Conflicts

S ally remembers a time of real agony from her childhood. It wasn't the divorce of her parents, although that was very painful for her. It wasn't when she was nine and her mother remarried, although that, too, was troublesome for her. It occurred some years later when she wrestled with conflicting feelings.

Let's backtrack just a bit. Although she spent only a couple of weeks during the summer and Christmas holidays with her father (who lived in another state), Sally felt very close to him. In time, however, she also became very attached to her stepfather, depending on him for the day-to-day things a father typically does. And this is when her agony began. She recalls:

> "I decided that I wanted to call my stepfather 'Dad,' but the word just stuck in my throat for many months. Every time I started to say it I felt overwhelmed by feelings of disloyalty to my biological father whom I also loved very much. I thought that if I loved my stepfather enough to call him Dad, I wouldn't be loving my real father as much any more. You can't imagine the distress that I went through until I finally found a solution."

Such feelings of mixed loyalties are common in stepfamilies and can slow the forging of new relationships. Not only are the loyalties of children like Sally strained, but those of parents and spouses as well. To understand the challenge of divided loyalties and ways to master the challenge, we begin by looking at the meaning and importance of family loyalty.

FAMILY LOYALTY

We value and admire loyalty. During World War II, after Buckingham Palace was bombed, reporters asked Elizabeth, the Queen Mother, when her daughters would leave England. She told them that her children would not leave until she did, that she would not leave until the King did, and that the King would not leave under any circumstances whatsoever. Such loyalty to duty and family was an inspiration to the English people during the dismal days of the war.

This kind of loyalty—a tenacious commitment to others—can develop in stepfamilies. Family loyalty tends to be strong because of the way it develops and the needs it fulfills.

1) Loyalty arises out of the bonding experience. A new-born baby's crucial psychological needs must be met if the infant is to develop properly. The most primary need is the need for secure attachment with another person. Typically, this attachment is initially with the mother. Psychologists give the name "bonding" to the process of forming this attachment. Bonding takes place as the mother is affectionate and responsive to the baby's needs for food and comfort.

Bonding is an emotional attachment. The mother and child fall in love with each other. As the infant develops, she will bond with other people as well, including her father, siblings, and grandparents. And the result is loyalty. The old adage "blood is thicker than water" is the observation that loyalty develops between family members that is stronger than in any other relationship.

2) Loyalty reflects your need to feel good about those closest to you. Recall that your identity is closely tied up with your intimate relationships. You need to feel good about your parents, your spouse, your children, your siblings, and others. That is, you need to feel that they are decent, competent, likeable, and caring individuals because they are a part of who you are. If you don't feel good about your family, it's more difficult to feel good about yourself.

This is one reason why people will remain loyal to family members under very trying circumstances. We have seen people defend and excuse family members who have lied or cheated or behaved badly in other ways. They do so because they are loyal. And they are loyal, in part, because they have a need to feel good about the people who are an important part of their own identity.

3) Loyalty means both responsibilities and benefits. Of course, loyalty isn't primarily about denying the faults of others. Loyalty entails both responsibilities and benefits for each family member because a family is a group of people committed to mutual support.

In a family, you are responsible to give, and you can expect to receive, whatever kind of support is needed—emotional, physical, financial, etc. One of the questions we raise when counseling someone who is experiencing difficulties is whether any family lives nearby. Family members are expected to help each other. In fact, "Whoever does not provide for relatives, and especially for family members, has denied the faith and is worse than an unbeliever" (1 Timothy 5:8).

4) Loyalty doesn't always develop, but when it does . . . By this point you probably have thought of someone who doesn't have the kind of family loyalty we have described. Indeed, some families don't work well. Or certain members of a family—such as siblings, or a parent and a particular child—have never bonded with each other in a way that results in loyalty.

Once established, the loyalty that grows out of bonding is very difficult to break. Loyalty is not merely a matter of obligation; it is something you need and desire. You are a loyal family member not just because you ought to be but also because you need and want to be.

Thus, when Sally agonized over whether she would be betraying her biological father, she was struggling with more than a sense of obligation. She was struggling because of her need and desire to retain her bond with him. She also had a need and desire to affirm her stepfather. To betray either one of them was unthinkable. Fortunately, she found the solution by talking with her biological father about her feelings. "You've always called me 'Daddy,'" he reminded her. "Go ahead and call him 'Dad.' That way we'll each have a special name."

LOYALTY CONFLICTS IN STEPFAMILIES

From the preceding, it is obvious why loyalty conflicts are both common and painful in stepfamilies. The nature of the conflict, however, is a little different for various stepfamily members.

1) Loyalty Conflicts For Children. The major loyalty conflict for children is between the stepparent and the same-sex parent. As with Sally, children may believe that loving a stepmother or stepfather is a betrayal of their mother or father. Such loyalty conflicts are not only common for children, they also tend to be recurring.

Sometimes a child will begin by calling a stepparent by his or her first name, then start saying "Mom" or "Dad," only to revert to the stepparent's first name again. This, of course, is distressing to a stepparent. But look at it from the child's viewpoint. For the child who has bonded with both biological parents, accepting someone else as a parent clearly smacks of disloyalty. It seems like a betrayal, a way of saying to your biological parent, "I no longer accept you as my parent. The love I reserved for you is now given to my stepparent." And even though most stepparents don't expect or want their stepchildren to stop loving their biological parents, it's the child's understanding of the situation that shapes his or her behavior.

In some cases, the stepparent does a better job of parenting than the biological parent. The stepchild may recognize this and use it to resolve loyalty conflicts, but you should avoid pointing out to a child the superior parenting skills of the stepparent. Remember, we all have a need to feel good about our parents.

We worked with a stepfamily in which, in our judgment, the stepmother did a much better job of parenting than had the biological mother. The biological mother was a drug abuser who largely allowed her son and daughter to do as they pleased. David, the son, told us about his struggle to maintain a relationship with his mother:

> "When my father divorced my mother, my sister, Dana, and I lived with him. A few years after the divorce, my mom finally stopped using drugs. But she still didn't lead the kind of life my father approved of. She had a lot of boyfriends and didn't keep house very well. In fact, her house is still pretty much of a mess compared to my father and stepmother's home.
>
> "Dana and I started visiting mom occasionally after she stopped using drugs. And now since I'm in college, I try to spend equal time with my mom and my dad and stepmother when I come home for a break. My dad really resents this. He tells me that my stepmother has been more of a mother to me than my mom ever has. He says I should respect my stepmother for all she's done for me. He thinks I ought to spend my time with him and my stepmother and only go to my mother if there is time to spare.
>
> "In some ways, my dad's right. My stepmother has been very good to me, and I really like her. But I'm afraid to get too close to her. I don't want to be cut off from my mother. I know she hasn't always been the best mother, but I also know she loves me. And she is my mother."

David expressed the dilemma children face as they struggle with loyalty conflicts well. With good insight, he recognizes that he is literally afraid of allowing himself to feel too close to his stepmother. He feels a duty, a need, and a desire to maintain a strong bond with his mother. At this point, he still doesn't see a way to do that and at the same time forge a close bond with his stepmother.

Unfortunately, David's struggle is intensified and prolonged by his father's insistence that David's loyalty to his mother is a form of disloyalty to his father and stepmother. David's father is maintaining a loyalty conflict that could be resolved. And he's doing so because he doesn't understand David's need to remain bonded with his biological mother.

2) *Loyalty Conflicts for Stepparents.* Stepparents who also have biological children typically experience loyalty conflicts. Regardless of the living arrangements—whether your children, stepchildren, or both live with you or another parent or stepparent—you are likely to face times when you feel torn between your deeply-imbedded loyalty to your own children and your developing loyalty to your stepchildren.

Loyalty conflicts for stepparents emerge from various situations. One situation involves giving love. Even if you have a good relationship with your stepchildren, you may find yourself having the same feelings as Corrine:

> "We have a difficult situation. My husband and I each brought children to this marriage. And the children are all close in age and all live with us. For the most part, we get along very well. I want my two stepchildren to feel loved. But I can't escape from the feeling that my own children are my real family. And I can't seem to help favoring them emotionally.
>
> "My husband and I didn't have any trouble adjusting to and becoming a part of each other's extended families. In fact, getting to know each other's brothers, sisters, parents, and cousins has been a smooth and gratifying process. I felt warmly welcomed by his family, and he felt the same about mine. But in spite of this, if I'm really honest, I have to admit that I still feel that my own children are my real children."

Although she doesn't realize it, Corrine is experiencing a loyalty conflict. She probably won't ever feel exactly the same about her stepchildren as she does about her own children. Moreover, she doesn't have to. But she does need to be aware that she is anxious about depriving her own children of love by loving her stepchildren.

Another situation that loyalty conflict takes for stepparents is financial support (we'll deal in greater detail with financial matters in chapter 8). Do you provide as much financial support for your stepchildren as for your own children? The question may seem easy to answer until you add some additional considerations. For example, what if your stepchild receives significant support from a biological parent? What if your stepchild doesn't live in your home but only visits on occasion? What if your stepchild expects to receive an inheritance some day? What if you are convinced that the money your spouse sends for support of your stepchild is squandered by the ex?

Take Corrine's situation once again. One of her complaints is that her husband gives money to his children too quickly and freely:

> "All they have to do is ask, and he gives them whatever they want without blinking an eye. I don't think they always need the money. And I definitely think they should provide good reasons why they need the money before he dishes it out."

Corrine's husband is not being partial to his children at the expense of his stepchildren. "He's a very generous man," she admits, "and will give my children whatever they want as quickly as he gives it to his own." But because Corrine's children do not ask as often, they receive less.

Corrine is experiencing another loyalty conflict. She appreciates her husband's generosity. She doesn't begrudge her stepchildren getting money. At the same time, she resents the fact that her stepchildren get more than her children get. Her resentment, in other words, grows out of her desire to protect her children's interests.

Time is another issue that produces loyalty conflicts for stepparents (we also talk more about this issue in chapter 8). How much time do you spend with your children and stepchildren? If your schedule is already packed, and you have too few hours with your own children, time spent picking up after, entertaining, and chauffeuring about your stepchildren can be quite vexing.

The issue of time can also create a conflict between loyalty to your stepchildren and loyalty to yourself. Should you spend time helping your stepchild with homework when you desperately need to relax? Should you take the time to cultivate your relationship with your stepchild when you have pressing obligations with work and household tasks? There are no simple answers to such questions. But, as we shall discuss below, there are some general ways to deal with loyalty conflicts that can help you find answers.

3) Loyalty Conflicts For Spouses. The major loyalty conflict for spouses is one of commitment—commitment to each other versus commitment to children and stepchildren. Nurturing your marriage is crucially important to building a successful stepfamily. It's so important, in fact, that we devote all of chapter 10 to this topic. In a first marriage, couples usually have some time to work on their relationship before they have children. However, a second marriage where children are involved doesn't allow for such a luxury. Coming into a stepfamily may feel like jumping on a moving train; all you can do, it seems, is hold on for dear life.

In other words, the loyalty conflict is rooted in the fact that you have limited time and resources to deal with the many challenges you face. A stepmother described her marital relationship with a tinge of regret in her voice, "All too often we have a minimum of time for each other. We're working on making more time for us, but we haven't figured out how to do it yet."

Loyalty conflicts also occur, and are more intense, when there are strained relationships in the stepfamily. A father described his painful situation:

"My daughter is at a stage in her life when she needs my support—not financial, but emotional support. And this requires a fair amount of time because she doesn't live with us. My wife—her stepmother—is not close to my daughter. They got along well at first but over the years they have drifted apart. My wife thinks that my daughter is manipulative and doesn't want me to spend any extra time with my daughter.

"So I'm caught in the middle. I also have another daughter by my present wife. She needs me. My wife needs me. And my oldest daughter needs me. What do I do?"

This man has the difficult dilemma of dealing with three people who need his loyalty. He can say about each one of them, "I ought to be loyal; I need to be loyal; I want to be loyal." But he can't see a way to be loyal to all of them. If he gives time to one, it takes time from the other. For now, he struggles. We don't know how it will turn out. We believe in the power of grace to be sufficient for every need. Hopefully, he does too.

4) Loyalty Conflicts For Grandparents and Other Relatives. Mae is a grandmother with a great deal of grace. Her son and daughter-in-law divorced after eight years of marriage and two children. A few years later, her daughter-in-law remarried and has another child by her second husband. Mae has maintained a close relationship with her ex-daughter-in-law and grandchildren. She thinks of the new baby as a her "grandchild" and treats him just like she does her biological grandchildren.

Many grandparents have difficulty being as impartial as Mae. Grandparents who show favoritism towards their biological grandchildren over their stepgrandchildren are a common problem in stepfamilies. Consider Heather's experience:

"When I married my first husband, we moved to the East Coast because of his work. This meant we were no longer near either of our families. A few years after our son was born, my husband had an affair and asked for a divorce. I was awarded custody of our son and my husband received liberal visiting rights. The combination of these rights and my job kept me on the East Coast. I met Matt, my second husband, at the hospital where I work. Matt has been a great stepfather to my son as well as a wonderful father to our two daughters.

"Matt grew up in this city, so his parents are nearby. His parents have been very good to me and have accepted my son as a grandchild—of sorts. But it's very clear that they favor their own grandchildren over my son. And he's old enough to recognize their favoritism.

"This is probably the worst thing in my life right now. I cherish the memories I have of times I spent with my own grandparents. My son is missing that. He sees my parents once or twice a year and his father's parents even less often. But sometimes I think he would be better off if he wasn't around my husband's parents at all."

These grandparents have a problem which is similar to Corrine's—they think of Heather's son as a nice young man and of her daughters as their real grandchildren. Their primary loyalty, therefore, is to their granddaughters.

Having children with two different spouses is one that causes turmoil in many stepfamilies. Consider the following scenario. Bob and Mindy have three children. They divorce, and Mindy marries Todd. A year later, Mindy is pregnant. She and Todd announce the pregnancy to her, Todd's, and Bob's families. She is startled by the amount of negative reaction she gets. After all, isn't a baby a cause for rejoicing? Isn't this baby an indication of the commitment that Todd and Mindy have to each other and to their stepfamily?

Why so much negative reaction? Mindy's three children are concerned about their mother's and their stepfather's reactions to the birth. Will the baby be favored over them because it will be their child? For Mindy's parents who still resent the divorce, the new baby ends any hope that Mindy and Bob will eventually get back together again. For Bob and his family, the baby is a reminder that Mindy's present joy is at the expense of his happiness (he hasn't remarried) and a signal that relationships with his children may be more complicated in the future. And even some of Todd's family are not thrilled with the news—they believe that Todd already has more than he can handle with three stepchildren.

Under such circumstances, it is not surprising that Todd and Mindy are surrounded by people experiencing loyalty conflicts. What can you do when you experience such conflict yourself, or when you live around others who are experiencing them?

MASTERING THE CHALLENGE OF LOYALTY CONFLICTS

As the stories we have shared in this chapter illustrate, loyalty conflicts are painful. Fortunately, there are a number of things you can do to deal with them:

1) Behave impartially even when you feel partial. One thing that helped Corrine deal with her loyalty conflict was to treat her children and stepchildren equally in spite of the fact that she regarded her children as her real family. What often happens in such cases is that behavior will pull feelings into line. George, who is a grandparent and a stepgrandparent, learned this when his wife insisted that he make no distinctions between biological grandchildren and stepgrandchildren:

> "I liked our stepgrandchildren, and I thought I had accepted them into the family. But when my wife and I went Christmas shopping that first year after we had stepgrandchildren, I realized that she was spending as much money on them as she was on our grandchildren. I pointed this out to her. She looked at me as if I were crazy, and said that of course we would spend as much on them. 'We'll treat them no differently from our other grandchildren,' she said.
>
> "Somehow, I just didn't expect to have to do everything for the stepgrandchildren that we did for the others. I thought my wife was being overzealous. But we've kept doing it. And now I can't imagine doing it any differently. I really think of those stepgrandkids as my own."

What George learned was a fact well known to social psychologists: you can change your attitudes and your feelings by controlling your behavior. If you feel a loyalty conflict, act as though there is no such conflict. In other words, be loyal to everyone. You may find that your feelings change, that eventually you will no longer feel the conflict. In any case, for the sake of stepfamily well-being, it is crucial to behave impartially even when you feel partial.

To behave impartially, incidentally, does not necessarily mean to treat everyone exactly the same. Parents relate to each child a little differently, whether the child is their own or a stepchild. As we shall see later, for example, you may be the primary disciplinarian for your own children but not for your stepchildren. You may do different sorts of things with your children and your stepchildren. To be impartial does not mean to be oblivious to differing needs and interests and circumstances.

2) Be sensitive to loyalty conflicts and avoid behavior that creates and/or prolongs them. We have given examples in this chapter of people who actually prolong loyalty conflicts by their behavior. Recall David's struggle, which his father prolonged by insisting that David should be more grateful to his stepmother than to his mother. His father wanted to resolve David's conflict, but he only intensified the problem by making demeaning remarks about David's mother.

Among the kinds of behavior that create or prolong loyalty conflicts are:

- talking disparagingly about a child's biological parent

- showing favoritism

- trying to speed up the bonding process

- insisting that loyalty to someone else is disloyalty to you

- making unfavorable comparisons between steprelations and biological relations

3) Be proactive in educating stepfamily members and other relatives about helpful behavior. Too often, even when aware of loyalty conflicts, people allow them to go on without confronting the behavior that is perpetuating them. It may not be easy to deal with such behavior, particularly when it involves others. Is your mother-in-law approachable? Will your uncle listen to reason? Would your parents be willing to change their behavior? Are your children or stepchildren old enough to handle a discussion? Such questions may make you hesitate to be proactive. You can balance them, however, by asking yourself how long you are willing to allow a loyalty conflict to detract from the quality of your stepfamily and your life.

Your approach, of course, will depend on who it is that needs guidance. Even at a young age, for example, you can talk to children about their feelings. Avoid a negative approach, such as, "What's wrong with you?" Rather, be positive by saying something like, "I know this is a hard time for you. Would you like to talk about it?" Or, "A lot of stepchildren worry because they think their stepmother is trying to take the place of their mother. But your mom will always be your mom. And your stepmother will do her best to help you when you're not with your mom. Maybe you can tell me how she can help."

Adults also may need guidance in how to be helpful to the stepfamily. Heather, for instance, is making a mistake by saying nothing to her in-laws or to her husband about the clear favoritism her in-laws show to her daughters over her son. If this is the worst thing happening in her life, why should she remain silent? She needs to talk about it with her husband and enlist his aid in confronting his parents.

In addition to your spouse, you may be able to get another family member to help educate others. George's wife, for example, is the kind of sensitive, caring person who is a good resource for educating other members of the family.

Note that we are speaking about "educating." If your approach is "I'm going to tell you how you ought to behave," you will probably run into resistance and resentment. On the other hand, if you approach someone with "It would really be helpful to our family if you could . . ." you are much more likely to get a favorable response.

4) Work to make your emotional divorce as complete as possible. Usually a stepfamily involves one or two people who have been divorced. Most divorced people we know agree that legal matters are vexing but that the emotional turmoil can be devastating. People who are legally divorced are not necessarily emotionally divorced. A therapist friend of ours, in fact, has coined the term "emotional polygamy" to refer to people who are married again but still emotionally tied to an ex-spouse.

Your emotional ties to your ex can be both positive and negative. Positive emotions include sympathy, feelings of responsibility for the ex's well-being, lingering sexual attraction, and admiration. Negative emotions include anger, jealousy, disdain, and resentment.

The problem with any emotional ties—whether positive or negative—is that they can create and prolong loyalty conflicts in your stepfamily. For example, Charles feels sympathy for the struggles of his ex-wife who has not remarried. He still feels some responsibility for her well-being. She calls him once in a while to come to her house and make a repair or help her with financial matters. Charles' present wife is piqued by the requests, and doesn't want him to go. She argues, "The children and I need you as much as she does."

Charles now has a loyalty conflict. Because he is still emotionally tied to his ex-wife he is torn between her requests and those of his present wife. It doesn't occur to him to advise his ex-wife to simply call a repairman or a neighbor to help. He could even offer to pay for the help. Such action might make him feel guilty at first, but in the long run it would help sever those emotional ties.

Or consider the way in which negative emotions can affect loyalty conflicts. We have known people who remain bitter for decades, or even for the remainder of their lives, after divorce. Such bitterness not only mars their own well-being but can perpetuate loyalty conflicts in their children. In fact, one of the problems that David's father has is that he is bitter about his ex-wife, feeling that she betrayed him and their children with her drug habit. He is bitter about the years of agony he endured as he tried to help her and keep the family intact. And the bitterness emerges in the negative statements he makes about her, statements which fuel David's loyalty conflict.

An emotional divorce doesn't mean that you will have no feelings at all about your ex-spouse. That's probably impossible. In any case, it is not necessary. Rather, an emotional divorce means that you no longer have either positive or negative feelings that interfere with your present life and contribute to loyalty conflicts.

Spouses can help each other recognize emotional ties to an ex. And they can help each other deal with them by discussing them and exploring ways to deal with them. For instance, Charles' wife could help him by pointing out that he could advise his ex to call someone else for assistance. And David's stepmother could help his father by reminding him of David's need to maintain a relationship with his mother.

If helping each other isn't sufficient, counseling may be needed. There may be some lingering issues that only a counselor can help you discover. Whatever it takes, it is worth the effort to make the emotional divorce as complete as possible.

5) Reassure your spouse, children, and stepchildren of your loyalty. Because the fear of loss often fuels loyalty conflicts, reassure your spouse, children, and stepchildren of their importance to you. And if you are the one needing reassurance, don't hesitate to ask for it. Here is a stepmother's story:

> "I know that my husband doesn't have romantic feelings for his ex-wife, but for a long time it rankled me every time we had to see her. I know I overreacted, but I just couldn't seem to help it. I would get edgy and irritable, and withdraw from my husband and spend more time with my children and stepchildren. My

husband knew the reason and he got annoyed with me. He reminded me that he still had legal obligations to his ex-wife that he could-
n't avoid and that I should grow up. I, of course, would get angry
and tell him that my feelings were natural and that he was being
unfair. But he said I needed to get counseling because it was my
problem.

"I knew he was right about it being my problem. But we didn't
see her that often, so I didn't see any point in getting counseling.
After an argument in which he got very angry at me, I started
thinking about it. When we were both calm, I asked him to talk
with me about it. As we talked, I realized that I was basically jealous
of his past relationship with her and anxious that she might win
back his affection. I told him so. And he told me that it would never
happen because he was happier with me than he ever had been
with her. I told him I thought that was all I needed to hear. But I
might need to hear it again when we had to see her.

"The next time we were scheduled to see his ex, he reminded
me of our conversation and of his commitment and love for me. I
still felt a few twinges, but it really hasn't been a problem since
then."

Children also need reassurance. Yet they may not ask for it. They
may act out their anxiety or resentment by sulking, lapsing into
silence, or misbehaving. Whenever you see such behavior, begin dealing with it by reassuring the child that he or she is one of the most
important people in your life. Your reassurance can take the form of
words: "I love you so much that I want you to be really happy. But you
don't seem very happy right now. Can I do anything to help?" It can
also take the form of action, "How about you and me doing something special together, just the two of us?"

You may find that the most effective help requires both words
and actions. A divorced father noticed his daughter becoming with-
drawn after he married a woman with two children of her own. He
realized that the daughter feared that she was no longer as important
to him. He also realized that his daughter was beginning to have a
loyalty conflict. On the one hand, she wanted to maintain a close rela-

tionship with him. On the other hand, she feared that she was losing him anyway and didn't want to continue emotionally investing herself in him.

He discussed the matter with his wife, and they agreed that he should try to spend some time alone with his daughter. The next weekend when his daughter came to stay with them, he took her out alone for a day. As they talked together, his daughter relaxed and became more open. These special days together became a regular practice for them. He also began calling her during the week to remind her that he loved her and to tell her how much he enjoyed their time together. These reassuring words and actions renewed and enhanced their relationship.

6) Be explicit with children about your expectations for step-relationships; repeat as needed. Be clear with your children that you don't expect their stepparent to replace their parent. Let them know that their stepsiblings will not change their status or importance with you. Just hearing these words from you will reassure your children and help them deal with a potential or actual loyalty conflict.

Therefore, if a child is struggling with a loyalty conflict, lay out the expectations and affirmations along the following lines (using, of course, language appropriate to the child's age) and repeat as often as needed:

• No one will replace your parents.

• No one will displace you.

• We don't expect you to feel the same way about your stepparent or stepsiblings as you do about your natural parent or siblings.

• We will do whatever we can to help you stay close to both your parents.

• We want you to let us know when you feel that you are being shortchanged in any way.

7) Whenever possible, be willing to go the second mile to help children resolve their loyalty conflicts. Jesus gave us this principle by which we are to live: "And if anyone forces you to go one mile, go also the second mile" (Matthew 5:41). In other words, as you try to help your children deal with a loyalty conflict, be prepared to give more than you receive and to accommodate the child's preferences, even though those preferences may sometimes involve additional time and effort.

It will help you to go the second mile if you keep in mind that they don't choose to feel a loyalty conflict and they certainly don't enjoy it. Also keep in mind that some of your best help may come as you go the extra mile for them.

Listen to the way Brett and his wife used the second-mile principle to help his youngest stepchild:

> "I married a woman with three children. I'd never had any children of my own, so I was thrilled about having a family. The two older children and I got along really well from the start. Cindy, her youngest, was a different matter. She clearly resented me, because she was really close to her dad. My wife and I decided to go the second mile to help her whenever we could.
>
> "We got our chance when school started. My wife drove the kids to school. The oldest two were in one school, and the youngest was in another. When my wife was married before, her husband drove the kids to school. Because of our work schedules, it was easier for me to take over that task than it was for my wife.
>
> "The two oldest had no problem with this arrangement. But Cindy said she didn't want me to drive her; she wanted her mother to do it. Explanations about the inconvenience didn't phase her. My wife and I agreed that this was a second-mile situation. She arranged her work so she could drive Cindy to school. I drove the other two. Six months later, my wife asked Cindy if I could drive her to school. She refused. After another three months, she asked Cindy again. To our surprise and relief, she agreed."

You may not be able to go the second mile in every situation. Fortunately, Brett's wife was able to adjust her schedule to accommodate Cindy. And it helped Cindy to deal with her loyalty conflict. Going the second mile for someone usually isn't easy. Sometimes it isn't even possible, however, when it is possible and you do it, it can work wonders.

The Ex Factor
The Challenge of Former Spouses

In the previous chapter, we noted that many people who are legally divorced are not necessarily emotionally divorced. They are caught in the uncomfortable condition of emotional polygamy—remarried but still emotionally tied to an ex-spouse. This condition can be deadly for stepfamily life.

Some people fixate on their divorces, constantly asking who was at fault and what could have prevented them. Others feel intense, chronic anger. Still others continue to think about their ex-spouses in larger-than-life terms by exaggerating either positive or negative attributes.

This is what happened to Louise and Trevor. Louise had been divorced for nearly two years when she met Trevor, who was also divorced. They quickly fell in love and were married within six months. Although neither had initiated their divorces, both felt they had learned a good deal from their failed first marriages. Both were ready for a permanent relationship and were determined to make marriage work the second time around. In one way, they had it easier than many stepfamilies. Louise had no children, and Trevor shared custody of his son with his ex-wife. Nevertheless, within five months their marriage was seriously threatened.

Their biggest problem was that Louise constantly compared Trevor to her ex-husband, Sam. Louise recalls:

"Almost from the moment I said 'I do,' I began to see things in Trevor that reminded me of Sam—for example, Sam's tendency to take me for granted. Trevor was really attentive when we were dating, but on our honeymoon I noticed a change. He called his office three times to check on business. Each time, I got furious. I began to wonder if he was going to be just like Sam.

"When we got home, things just got worse. For starters, Trevor seemed more interested in opening the mail than in looking at our honeymoon pictures. I got mad and accused him of behaving like Sam. He couldn't understand my reaction and accused me of being unreasonable.

"The first weekend we were home from our honeymoon, Trevor's son stayed with us. I knew I had to be a good sport about this, but I was angry because of the time and attention Trevor gave his son. It reminded me of the way Sam would ignore me when his brother came to visit us and I would feel like a nuisance.

"Every time Trevor did something that reminded me of Sam, I lost my cool. Our relationship was going down the tubes faster than it had come together. In desperation, Trevor and I made a determined effort to sort things out. And it finally dawned on me, after some intense discussions with Trevor and a close friend, that I was married to one man but emotionally tied to another. I was still angry with Sam, and I was taking it out on Trevor."

Fortunately, Louise resolved her anger with the help of counseling and support from Trevor. Happily, her second marriage is flourishing.

Responsibilities as well as emotional ties to an ex-spouse can also present a problem. You may find yourself, for example, altering your own schedule to accommodate your ex (and perhaps your ex's new wife and stepchildren) as you deal with matters concerning your children. You have to consult your ex when you want to take the children on vacation, when they are having problems in school, or when they need orthodontics. And the list goes on. Legally, the divorce is final, but in terms of emotions, time, energy, and finances, it continues.

EMOTIONAL TIES THAT ARE BINDING

If you and your ex have children, he or she will always be a part of your life. At the very least, you will see something of your ex in your children. At the most, your ex can imperil your new family.

As Louise and Trevor illustrate, emotional ties to an ex can be particularly trying. They have worked through that problem. Yet many others, like Tim and Jean, are not so fortunate. Tim's ex-wife, Monica, seems like a constant presence in their marriage. Because they share custody of their three children, Tim and Monica are in frequent contact. Jean suspects that Monica would like to make the contact permanent. She is always calling Tim for advice or asking him to fix something around the house. And Tim is quick to oblige her. Jean is fed up with Monica's intrusion in their lives and wants Tim to limit all but the necessary communication between them.

The two cases—Louise and Trevor on the one hand, and Tim and Jean on the other—illustrate an important point: the trouble with your ex may be due to your feelings, your spouse's feelings, or both of your feelings. We have heard people say they hate their ex-spouses. We have heard people say they despise their spouse's ex. And we have heard couples agree that they both detest one or both of their ex-spouses.

You may think of such feelings as a personal problem, but not as an issue in your present marriage. However, Louise and Trevor illustrate how anger towards an ex can contaminate a second marriage. Positive feelings or habits picked up from an ex can have similar results. One man discovered this when he and his second wife differed about the use of place mats on their kitchen table. He insisted they were essential; she insisted that they were nice but not necessary. They had several intense arguments before they resolved the issue. As it turned out, he had learned the practice from his first wife. He had a strong feeling that the place mats were important. But he finally realized that his feelings reflected a tie to his ex rather than a well-thought-out conviction of his own.

Our intimate relationships affect everything from our identity to our living habits. It is unlikely that you could live with a person for a number of years without carrying residual effects of that relationship into your second marriage. Of course, some of these effects may actually enhance the quality of your second marriage. Even in marriages that fail, spouses often pick up some useful interpersonal skills from each other. Unfortunately, however, other effects of your first marriage may be potentially destructive for your second marriage. Thus, as we pointed out in the last chapter, it is important to make the emotional divorce as complete as possible.

BEHAVIOR THAT IS TROUBLESOME

In addition to emotional ties, the contact you still have with your ex, or the contact your spouse has with an ex, may be distressing. Let's look at the way the behavior of an ex-spouse can be a problem to those trying to forge a satisfying stepfamily life.

1) The ex doesn't fulfill obligations to your children. This is one of the most infuriating kinds of behavior from an ex. It can take many forms—from showing up late to pick up the children to skipping the monthly support check. A typical reaction is, "It's one thing to hurt me. But how could he hurt his own children?" Actually, in some cases, the behavior is meant to hurt the ex rather than the children. The father who shows up late to pick up a child, for instance, may do so to irritate his ex-wife. The mother who doesn't have the children ready when the father arrives may be trying to punish him. The father who misses an outing may regret the time not spent with his child but silently enjoy the thought of his ex waiting and fuming.

In other words, the failure to fulfill obligations is frequently not a lack of responsibility but a tactic in the ongoing war with the ex. If there's no business like show business, there's also no anger like a divorcee's anger. And that anger manifests itself in various kinds of behavior meant to punish the ex. Unfortunately, the behavior winds up punishing the children as well.

We don't mean to imply that the "ongoing war" is a conscious, carefully planned operation. Even people who are generally decent and kind are often driven by anger to act in punitive ways toward an ex. And they would be horrified by the realization that their children are also victims of this behavior.

*2) **The ex frustrates your current plans.*** It may be anything from a weekend trip to the purchase of a new home. But your ex does something, or fails to do something, that frustrates these plans. Here, too, his or her actions may be a result of anger. They may also reflect the circumstances of your ex's life; remember that stepfamily life is more complicated because more people are involved.

For example, Abe and Patrice were frustrated by her ex because he kept delaying the final settlement of their property. Patrice's ex-husband was to give her half of the profit he made from selling a piece of vacation property they jointly owned. Abe and Patrice planned to use the money to pay for a European vacation with their new stepfamily. But the ex first "forgot" to put the property up for sale, then was "too busy" for awhile to show it to anyone, and then couldn't get a "decent price" for it. So instead of the trip to Europe, Abe and Patrice took their first vacation as a stepfamily at a nearby lake.

The behavior of Patrice's ex suggests a classic example of passive-aggressiveness. We believe that he—knowingly or unknowingly—was acting out his anger against Patrice by delaying the sale.

In contrast, the plans of another couple for a weekend trip alone was frustrated when the wife's ex-husband called to say he couldn't take care of the children. His wife's mother had been seriously ill, and they had to travel across the country to be with her. In this case, the complexities of stepfamily life, rather than anger, forced a change of plans.

*3) **The ex subjects your children to standards and values that differ from yours.*** This is a tough one. "Different" doesn't necessarily mean wrong. Still, it can be irritating if you believe that your child is being inappropriately influenced when spending time with your ex. Some of the complaints that people make about the standards and values of their exes include:

• "He has a woman living with him."

• "He drinks a lot around the children."

• "She's too permissive; she buys them anything they want."

• "Instead of telling them to wait until marriage, she tells them to use contraceptives if they have sex."

• "His new wife is a 'neat-freak' and watches every move the kids make; he won't do anything about it."

• "Her husband is too strict; even on Friday nights, he makes my daughter do her homework, without any help from him or my ex-wife, before she can do anything else."

The above list is only a sampling of the kinds of differences that people find troublesome. Clearly, some are more serious than others. But if you believe that your children are being adversely affected in any way, you are likely to find any difference vexing.

4) *The ex tries to sabotage your relationship with the children.* At the very least, your ex wants the children to prefer him or her to you. At the most, the ex wants the children to reject you. His or her tactics can range from insinuations to negative statements to ingratiating behavior. Again, such actions likely stem from anger.

Insinuations, which include gestures, are subtle put-downs. For example, when the children are with the ex, a question might be raised, "Does your mother have another boyfriend?" "Another" is meant to let the children know that she can't maintain a lasting relationship with one man. If the answer is yes, the father says, with a look of disgust, "It doesn't surprise me."

Negative statements are more direct. The ex-spouse may hammers away at the child about such things as faults of the mother or father, the deficiencies as a spouse and parent, or a lack of morality and sensitivity. In the long run, this abusive strategy probably will fail. Children are intelligent enough to make their own decisions about character. Moreover, the parent who has wrongly bad-mouthed the other will eventually fall in their estimation.

Ingratiating behavior is a way to contrast how you and your ex feel about the children. For example, the ex may lavish gifts on the children, take them places you can't afford, and generally treat them royally. This often is an attempt to say to the children, "See how much I love you? See how much more fun you have when you're with me?" Be careful in jumping to such a conclusion, however. Simply because your ex can afford to do things for the children that you can't doesn't necessarily mean that he or she is taking unfair advantage. Your ex may just enjoy spending the money on the children.

5) Your ex doesn't communicate with you. If it weren't for the children, of course, this would be a blessing. But when you share responsibility for your children, communication is an imperative. Some examples of how the lack of communication can be a problem include:

• "She didn't even tell me when my son was sick."

• "I don't know what goes on when the kids are with their father, and he won't tell me anything."

• "She planned the birthday party without asking me for my input on the time and place."

• "He decided on his own what to do about our daughter's college education; I wasn't even a part of the discussion."

Lack of communication may also reflect anger. Or it may result from practical difficulties, such as distance and schedules. In either case, both children and parents suffer when communication breaks down.

6) Your spouse resents your ex. Stepfathers may resent their wives' ex-husbands because the ex doesn't pay sufficient attention to the children or carry his share of the weight in dealing with their physical, emotional, and financial needs. Stepfathers may also resent what they regard as past or current mistreatment of their wives.

Such resentment can be intense. When the anger is rooted in a perceived lack of responsibility of the ex for his children, the stepfather may try to turn the children against their father. This is likely to backfire and only cause more problems in the stepfamily. It can be troublesome, even if the stepfather is entirely motivated by a desire to protect his stepchildren. One stepfather, who took actions to adopt his stepdaughter because he felt her father neglected her, was distressed to find that this action only alienated her. Even though she was angry and wanted little to do with her father at the time, she had no wish to be adopted by her stepfather.

Stepmothers also have problems with their husbands' ex-wives. They may resent the way ex-wives try to manipulate their husbands, sabotage their stepchildren's relationships with them, or interfere with the routines they are trying to establish in their stepfamilies. As a stepmother complained:

> "Every time my stepson comes back from his mother's house, I feel like I have to start all over with him. She spoils him and lets him do whatever he wants. There are no rules at her house, but we believe in rules. She's making our family life very difficult."

DEALING WITH YOUR EX BEFORE YOU EXPLODE

You may have seen something of your own situation in the various behaviors we have just described. Or you may have some issues with your ex not covered in our list. In either case, the following steps will be useful in dealing with your ex or your spouse's ex:

1) Come to terms with, and learn to control, your anger. As we have pointed out, many problems with an ex-spouse arise out of continuing anger. Of course, you don't choose to feel angry. And undoubtedly your ex-spouse has behaved or behaves in a way that makes your anger understandable. But just because your anger is understandable doesn't mean you can't deal with your anger. You can stop it from being what it is for too many people—a form of self-destructive behavior that damages not only the angry person but his or her relationships as well.

How, then, do you deal with your anger? First, you need to accept the fact that anger is a destructive emotion that you want to minimize in your life. As we remember from Ephesians 4:31: "Put away from you all bitterness and wrath and anger and wrangling and slander, together with all malice". So if you've got it, try to get rid of it—as quickly as you can (Ephesians 4:26).

"But," you may think, "how can I help it if I feel anger?" That's not the point. The point is to find ways to handle and minimize your anger. Here are some things you can do:

• Identify the source or sources of your anger. "That's easy," may be your reaction, "it's my ex." But, before you conclude that your ex is the sole cause of your anger, consider other possible sources, such as difficulties at work or with a stepchild. Blaming your ex for anger that has other sources only cripples you in your efforts to manage your anger well.

Even when you identify your ex as a source of your anger, get specific. What exactly is it about your ex or your ex's behavior that angers you? The answers to this question are important in helping you deal with your anger.

• Ask yourself what kind of changes would relieve your anger and what you can do to bring about those changes. When we ask people who are intensely angry towards an ex what change would relieve their anger, we sometimes get responses such as, "It would really help if he would move to a different planet." Since your ex is not likely to accommodate you by disappearing from the planet, how can you remedy his or her troublesome behaviors?

You may be able to modify some of those behaviors by negotiating or discussing them with your ex. And if that doesn't work, you may be able to alter the situation or change your own behavior. For example, if your ex is always late in picking up the children, discuss the matter with him or her. Find out whether there is a legitimate reason for the late arrival or whether it is your ex's anger that causes the behavior. Hopefully, your ex will respond by saying, "We're both angry, but let's try to stop hurting each other. Let's focus on one of the best things of our life together—our children—and work together to make their life as good as possible."

If your ex isn't amenable to discussion, you may be able to change the situation or yourself. For instance, you can decide that you will not be victimized, that you will simply plan on the children being picked up late, and that you will schedule your activities so that whatever time the children are picked up makes no difference in what you do.

There are other ways to minimize, or even to eliminate, your anger. Try some of these remedies and see if they work for you:

• Practice giving people the benefit of the doubt. If you practice with people in general, it will be easier to do it with your ex. If your ex is late picking up the children, perhaps there is a legitimate reason. If your ex is irregular with child payments, perhaps he or she is financially strapped.

If you assume the troublesome behavior is another example of irresponsibility or vengeance, you will only feel anger. On the other hand, if you avoid jumping to uninformed conclusions by assuming there may be an understandable reason for the behavior, you are less likely to be angry without cause.

• Find constructive ways to cool down. Everyone needs to cultivate constructive ways to cool down when anger strikes. What works for one person may not work for another, so discover what works for you. Some people use prayer, positive thinking, or exercise to diffuse anger. Others, unfortunately, resort to counterproductive methods, such as excessive drinking, extravagant purchases, or verbal abuse.

• Learn how to forgive. This is fundamental. In fact, it is so important—and sometimes so difficult—that we will discuss it in detail below.

2) Communicate and work with your ex on child-rearing issues. In general, communication between ex-spouses about the children is imperative. For those who have trouble being civil to each other, we recommend they begin by agreeing on the following:

• We have to talk with each other about our children's needs and problems.

• When discussing a child-rearing issue, we will not bring up any other topic.

• When discussing a child-rearing issue, we will strive to keep the children's well-being in mind and not use the children to battle each other.

• We shall conclude all discussions about our children by reviewing what we have agreed on so there is no misunderstanding later on.

Those who are able to be civil with each other have a great advantage, and their children will benefit. For instance, Trevor and Louise, whom you met at the beginning of this chapter, have a good relationship with Trevor's ex-wife and her second husband. Trevor's ex-wife calls him to discuss problems with their son when they occur. When their son started experimenting with cigarettes, Trevor's ex called him immediately. She was clearly distressed. Although his son stayed with him and Louise every other weekend, Trevor was unaware of his son's flirtation with cigarettes.

Trevor and Louise met with Trevor's ex and her husband to discuss the issue. They knew they had to work together to stop the boy from getting addicted to what all of them agreed was a destructive habit. Louise happily recounted the outcome:

"Trevor and his ex-wife still grate on each other. But when it comes to their son, they work like a team. They both love him very much, and it shows in the way they talk about him.

"So we agreed that when his son is at our house, Trevor and I would keep closer tabs on him to make sure he couldn't go somewhere and sneak a smoke. According to his mother, he had done this a couple of times. We also agreed that a positive approach is best. We don't want him to feel like we're always spying on him. So his mother and stepfather said they would sit down with him, explain why they didn't want him to smoke, and offer him a reward if he agreed to stop.

"We said we would talk with him the next time he was at our house, tell him we agree with his mother and stepfather completely, and that we would contribute to the reward so it could be something really special."

Such cooperation between the four adults responsible for parenting the boy serves everyone's interests.

Note that Louise pointed out that Trevor and his ex still do not get along like good friends, but they are able to act like friends when it comes to helping their son. Communicating and working with your ex on matters dealing with your children is not always possible. But don't assume it is impossible until you have made every effort to bring it about. The benefits are enormous, including:

• The children are parented by three—or possibly four—responsible adults, rather than by two sets of adults who pull the children in different directions.

• The children's world is more ordered, more stable, and more consistent, thereby enhancing their well-being.

• More minds are available to tackle the difficult decisions that must be made in child-rearing, thereby raising the potential for creative solutions.

• There is less likelihood of children manipulating the biological parents, or playing parents against each other, because the parents talk, rather than relying on their personal assumptions or on the children's reports.

• Anxiety about what will happen to children when they are at the other home will be lessened or eliminated.

• There is less likelihood of feeling shut out of the part of the children's lives that is spent with the other parent.

• The goodwill created by cooperation tends to reduce or eliminate anger you feel toward your ex.

Clearly, you, your children, your marriage, and your stepfamily all benefit from communicating and working with your ex.

Anything in your life that creates anger, anxiety, distaste, or distress in your life on an ongoing basis will detract from the quality of your present marriage and family life as well as from your personal well-being. The challenges of building a rewarding stepfamily are great enough without the added burden of having your energy, time, and positive moods assaulted by vexations with an ex-spouse.

3) Distinguish between matters of preference or style and matters of right and wrong. A common source of frustration for people in stepfamilies is the belief that the children are being exposed to wrong values, wrong attitudes, wrong behavior, and wrong expectations at the other home. Indeed, there are cases where this is true. But in our experience, the differences are often matters of preference or style rather than of right or wrong.

Consider the following examples. Would you judge them as right and wrong or as matters of preference or style?

• In his mother's home, John gets help with his homework every night. In his father's home, he is expected to do his homework on his own because "he will learn better that way."

• In her mother's home, Kelly can date now that she is fifteen. In her father's home, she must wait until she is older.

• In his mother's home, Dan has to wash the car every other week because this is the "responsible thing" to do. In his father's home, Dan doesn't have this responsibility because his father has the car washed at a service station.

• In her mother's home, Laurel bathes every night. In her father's home, Laurel bathes when she is dirty.

• In his mother's home, sixteen-year-old Chris has no curfew and his mother may be asleep by the time he comes home. In his father's home, Chris has a curfew of eleven o'clock, and his father is always up when he comes home.

• In her mother's home, Deanna always eats breakfast with the rest of the family. In her father's home, the family rarely has breakfast together and Deanna often skips breakfast.

You may believe that some of the examples are indeed moral matters, while others are matters of preference or style. Before concluding that something involves a question of right or wrong, however, you should discuss the matter with your spouse. You may decide that some of the differences, while repugnant to you personally, are not really moral issues. If so, remind yourself that your children are being exposed to diverse patterns of living, rather than to corrupting influences.

However, if you and your spouse agree that a moral issue is at stake, you need to discuss it with your ex. If your ex refuses to accept your point of view, discuss it with your pastor or counselor and determine what, if anything, should and can be done further about the matter.

4) Practice forgiveness. Forgiveness is central to our faith:

"As God's chosen ones, holy and beloved, clothe yourselves with compassion, kindness, humility, meekness, and patience. Bear with one another and, if anyone has a complaint against another, forgive each other; just as the Lord has forgiven you, so you also must forgive" (Colossians 3:12-13).

Frequently in our work with couples, we have been astonished at how many people seem unwilling to practice forgiveness. They do so to their own detriment. The lack of forgiveness can be spiritually destructive as well as toxic to personal well-being and to relationships.

We believe that one of the reasons people find it so difficult to forgive is that they misunderstand what it means. One New Testament word for forgiveness (used by Jesus in the Lord's Prayer and by Peter when he asked Jesus how often he should forgive those who wrong him) means to let go, to send away, give up, cancel, and pardon. The word used in the passage quoted above from Colossians means to give freely or graciously as a favor, or to pardon.

Putting the various meanings together, forgiveness is a gift to another person where you give up revenge or retaliation and cancel any debt or guilt. This is a much different meaning from the common forgive and forget. You can't erase from your memory the hurt you experienced with your ex, but you can graciously give it up and let it go.

Forgiveness also has a different meaning from one we have found commonly—that if you truly forgive someone, you will feel good about and like that person. But forgiveness does not necessarily make you like someone. It doesn't necessarily repair and restore the relationship, for forgiveness is unilateral—it is your gift to the other person. It is a gift that says, "I will not treat you as you have treated me, and I willingly cancel any debt you have to me." You can forgive someone, therefore, independently of what the other person does.

Feeling good about someone else and relating to that person as a friend, however, depends on what the other person does as well as what you do. For instance, let's say that you forgive your ex. But your ex's response is, in effect, "I haven't treated you badly. I'm not indebted to you. I have no reason to feel guilty." Such words doom reconciliation. They fail to acknowledge personal responsibility for your bro-

ken relationship and they indicate no desire to seek forgiveness—
the essential elements of reconciliation. As a result, you will still feel
estranged from your ex. You won't like him or her. You won't be his
or her friend.

So what is the point of forgiveness if it doesn't make you like
your ex as a person? The point is to gain release from bitterness and
resentment. In this sense, forgiveness is a gift to yourself as well as
to your ex. Forgiveness is a way of breaking away from the destructive emotions that still bind you to your ex. Forgiveness is liberation
from the past and an open door to a more fulfilling future.

Forgiveness also means liberation from a downward spiral of
destructive behavior. Vera, who has three stepchildren, was almost
caught in such a downward spiral. In this case, she found release in
forgiveness of her husband's ex:

> "My three stepchildren live with us. The youngest, a boy, got
> mixed up with the drug crowd in high school. He was caught sell-
> ing marijuana and was expelled from school. Stan, my husband,
> just went ballistic. Our whole family was in turmoil. It was an
> awful time for us.
>
> "Stan was angry, and I took the brunt of his anger. I, in turn,
> got angry with his ex-wife. One day I told Stan that she was the
> one who had messed up her son's life. This only made him more
> angry. He said we were the ones raising the kids and had to take
> the responsibility for their behavior.
>
> "I firmly believed then, and still believe, that Stan's ex was the
> cause of my stepson's problems. But as I prayed about it, I real-
> ized that it was no good to get angry at her or to blame her in
> front of Stan and the children. The past couldn't be erased. We
> had to deal with the present. And we couldn't deal very well with
> the present if we got stuck on blaming Stan's ex. So I forgave her.
> And to this day I have never again said anything against her."

Vera's forgiveness meant that she no longer focused on the
mother's role in causing the problem or retaliated by pointing out
her faults to Stan and the children. Her forgiveness also released
Vera from her bitterness. And we are happy to report that Stan and

Vera patiently worked with the boy; he is now well-adjusted, free of drugs, and on his way to a productive career.

In spite of the benefits, some people find it difficult to forgive. We suggest you consider the following questions if you are having trouble forgiving your ex or your spouse's ex:

• Have you told someone how, and how much, you were hurt? It's hard to forgive until you articulate your pain. It isn't necessary to express it to the person who hurt you; although, that usually helps. You can share your hurt with your spouse, with a pastor, with a trusted friend, with God in prayer. But you need to articulate your hurt before you will be able to forgive.

• Does the person you told fully understand your hurt? Have you ever shared a problem with someone, only to have the sense that the other person didn't really understand your feelings? When you share your pain, don't let the matter drop until you are convinced that the other person fully understands. If you have any doubts, have the person say back to you what you have told them, and have them express what you feel.

• Do you understand your own contribution to the problem? Most of us believe that we were treated unjustly when someone else hurts us. But in the case of intimate relationships, there is rarely a completely innocent victim. To acknowledge that you contributed to the problem with your ex will help you to affirm your common humanity and make it easier to practice forgiveness.

• Do you really want to forgive? We raise this question for a number of reasons. First, you may not want to forgive because you still want to punish your ex in some way. Second, you may not want to forgive in order to remind others how deeply you have been hurt. Third, you may not want to forgive because you enjoy fantasizing about terrible things happening to your ex. Fourth, you may not want to forgive because your ex continues to engage in annoying behavior.

Nevertheless, you have an obligation to forgive. It is a spiritual obligation because God commands it. It is a personal obligation because bitterness is self-destructive. It is a family obligation because negative emotions will contaminate your stepfamily life.

• How can your spouse help you? We have a fundamental principle of a good marriage: everything in marriage is a mutual responsibility. If you are having difficulty forgiving your ex or your spouse's ex, enlist your spouse's aid. Talk about what each of you can do to encourage forgiveness.

You should do whatever it takes to exercise forgiveness. Ironically, the very hurt that makes you reluctant to forgive will continue to gnaw at you until you do forgive. Forgiveness may not make you like your ex any more, but it will free you to attend to the important business of building a satisfying stepfamily life.

Can We Make It?
The Challenge of Resources

As a new stepmother discovered, there are times when you wonder if you have sufficient resources to deal with the challenge of stepfamily life:

"I married a man with five kids. I can't have children myself, so I was thrilled to have a ready-made family. I thought of us as a kind of Brady bunch, you know, the television stepfamily that always had a rousing good time. But that first summer, when the kids were all at home every day, I thought I would go crazy. We started spending more money than we should have just to get away from the house. By the end of the summer, I was exhausted. And I could only think of one thing—there would be another summer in nine more months and I wasn't sure if I could bear it."

Not many people, of course, are faced with a "ready-made family" with five children. Still, time, money, and energy all seem to be in relatively short supply for contemporary families of every kind. Often, the shortages are even more troublesome for stepfamilies. Most families, for example, experience occasional financial problems. In stepfamilies, the problem may be more severe because one or both of the partners has a monetary responsibility to a former family. This responsibility can pose a serious burden for the new family, limiting their economic well-being because a portion of their resources go to support the former family or families.

Time and energy are also at a premium because of the sheer number of people and demands in a stepfamily. A common complaint of stepparents is: "We don't have any time for ourselves as a couple. And when we do have time, we're too worn out to enjoy it."

We sympathize. But we believe that most couples have the necessary resources—including time, money, and energy—for building a satisfying stepfamily life. Let's look at the resources you need, the challenge that stepfamily life presents to the management of those resources, and ways you can use your resources to the greatest advantage.

EVERY FAMILY NEEDS RESOURCES

As far as the need for resources is concerned, stepfamilies are no different from biological families. As we'll discuss in the next section, the challenge of using those resources wisely may be more severe. But every family requires resources—including the important resources of time, money, social networks, and spiritual tools.

1) Time. You need time together to build your family identity. It has become popular to talk about the importance of quality time, rather than the sheer amount of time. We agree to an extent; yet, we have known people who try to justify the minimal amount of time they spend with their spouses, children, or stepchildren by asserting that it's "quality time."

To be realistic, quality time demands a sufficient quantity of time. Consider your own courtship. Would you now be married to your spouse if he or she had told you during your courtship that you could only spend ten minutes a week together because of other demands, but that it would be quality time? Probably not, because getting to know someone requires shared time and experiences. Of course, you can have a lot of time together that isn't quality time. Just as clearly, however, you can't possibly have quality time unless you have a certain quantity as well.

We hear people say, "I know I should spend more time with my family, but there just aren't enough hours in the day." In fact, you have just as much time as anyone—twenty-four hours each day. As we'll discuss later, however, you may need to manage your time more skillfully.

2) Money. When we talk about money as an important resource, someone often points out that money can't buy happiness. We respond, "Neither can poverty." The point of money is not to buy happiness, but to have enough to provide the family with four important things:

• Security from the threat of hunger and the loss of other basic needs.

• Freedom from painful choices (do we buy medicine or shoes?) and from the conflict that arises over those choices.

• The capacity to enjoy some of the many attractive offerings in our culture (from computer games to vacations).

• The opportunity to serve God by helping those who have less than you.

As with the issue of time, the problem for many people is not that they need more money, but that they need to manage more effectively the money they have. In many cases, effective management means accepting a standard of living consistent with current income. Or it could mean accepting a lower standard of living in order to manage both time and money more wisely. How will you profit by spending fifty to sixty hours a week working in order to maintain a standard of living higher than 95% of the world's population, if you lose your health or your stepfamily in the process?

3) Social network. Your social network includes your extended family and friends. It includes the people you see regularly and with whom you share activities and provide mutual support. These are the people who you turn to, and who turn to you, when you celebrate a special event, or when you want to spend a relaxing evening or weekend, or when you need some kind of help.

If possible, your network should include other stepfamilies so you can support each other in your unique struggles and triumphs. For instance, many stepfamilies find it useful to be part of stepfamily support groups at their churches or at local Stepfamily Association of America chapters. You may not see such people outside the group meetings, but they can be an important resource.

Your social network provides an important source of knowledge and insight for meeting the challenges of stepfamily life. There are times when the advice may be useless or even counterproductive. But other people, including family and friends, have confronted and resolved problems similar to yours, and you can profit from their experiences.

4) *Spiritual tools.* Spiritual tools are a resource for enhancing your stepfamily as well as your personal well-being. "I came," Jesus said, "that they may have life, and have it abundantly" (John 10:10). It's difficult to live a full, abundant life if your stepfamily is tearing you apart emotionally and physically. We believe, therefore, that the offer of abundant life includes the offer to help you forge a satisfying step-family life. Indeed, when we asked a stepmother to describe a way in which spiritual resources were important to her, she said:

> "Important isn't the word. Necessary is the word. In fact, it was my early experiences as a stepmother that drove me back to church. I just didn't think I could cope. But as I began to worship and pray again, I found myself learning how to handle my stepchildren."

This stepmother now has a strong marriage and a warm, loving relationship with her stepchildren.

THE CHALLENGE OF USING RESOURCES IN STEPFAMILY LIFE

You may have noticed that these four important resources are inter-related. In some ways, they even interfere with each other. For instance, if you need more time with your stepfamily but also need more money, you may struggle with getting a part-time job. Similarly, if you already feel pressed for time, expanding your social network or getting involved in church may intensify the problem.

The four resources can also overlap and support each other. For example, one couple found a way to draw on three of the resources at once. They volunteered to teach a Sunday School class in which her daughter (his stepdaughter) was enrolled. This gave them additional time with the girl, expanded their social network (by meeting and getting to know other teachers), and provided them with more spiritual tools (by grounding them more thoroughly in the teachings of their church and giving them an opportunity to serve).

As we noted earlier, the challenge of using the various resources well is common to all families. In stepfamilies, however, there are unique challenges that we need to consider:

1) Spending time with noncustodial children. A common complaint, particularly about noncustodial fathers, is that they do not spend sufficient time with their children. We hear such things as:

- "Their father rarely takes them or even sees them. This doesn't give my husband and me any time to be by ourselves."

- "Since he remarried, he doesn't seem to care about his children any more. I think he's written them off."

- "He was good at first. But, over time, he has had less and less contact with our daughter. It really hurts her."

Nearly half of the children of divorced parents who are asked report that they have not seen their fathers over the past year. From the fathers' point of view, this can happen for a variety of reasons:

• It is more painful to see the ex-wife than to not see the children.

• The father is involved with someone new and is spending all his time with her.

• The father is involved with someone new who doesn't want him to maintain close contact with his ex or his children.

• The father is remarried, has stepchildren, and has no time left for his own children after caring for his stepfamily.

• The father is convinced that his ex-wife has turned his children against him so that they no longer want to spend time with him.

You may not be convinced by such reasons. Nevertheless, the problem of time remains if you are the mother or stepfather in a stepfamily where the natural father has little or no contact with the children. One one level, it puts most or all of the parenting burden on you, making it more difficult for you to spend time together as a couple. On another, the children are likely to feel alienated from their father and in need of extra support from you. This requires that you give time to dealing with their feelings that you might have used to enjoy some kind of leisure activity together.

There's another level to the problem. If you are a noncustodial parent, you face the challenge of spending time with your children without neglecting your stepfamily. The problem is compounded if you believe that your children need time alone with you rather than in the context of your stepfamily.

These situations—where your stepchildren's parent has minimal contact with his or her children, or where you are the noncustodial parent who must find time to care both for your stepfamily and your children—are serious challenges to your time-management skills. We'll discuss those skills more fully below.

2) Making sure that financial resources are both adequate and fairly allocated. Much post-divorce bitterness focuses on money issues. Indeed, we have never talked to anyone who said, "The property distribution was fair—exactly what it should have been." Even if the property is divided equally, one or both parties may believe that their contribution or need is greater than that of their ex-spouse.

The property struggles in a divorce tend to carry over into the stepfamily. The divorcee, perceiving him- or herself to have been cheated by the divorce, is more sensitive to money issues and less tolerant of any further injustice. Here are some of the complaints and problems that people express about money in the stepfamily:

- "My wife and I can't agree on whether we need one, two, or three checking accounts. She thinks that one account would be a symbol of our commitment. But she has two children and I have one, and I think my son will be shortchanged if we have just one account."

- "Why should I have to pay for my stepson's college education when his father has more money than he knows what to do with?"

- "I know that my husband's ex spends some of the money he sends for child support on herself. And now he wants to send even more!"

- "We are really struggling financially. And the main reason we're struggling is that some of my income has to go to my husband's ex-wife and their children. She's supposedly too emotionally upset to work."

- "Because she has three kids and I have one, her kids get a lot more of our money than mine does. I know that each one gets about the same, but it still bothers me that so much of our money goes to my stepchildren."

• "I can't believe the amount of money he spends on his daughter. It's not because she needs it. He's buys her any-thing she wants because he feels so guilty about the divorce."

Such money issues can cause a good deal of anguish before they're resolved. No formula for resolution works for everyone. You can profit from knowing how other people have dealt with money problems. But, ultimately, you must find a solution that is satisfactory to each of you.

3) Stretching the resources to include "yours, mine, and ours."
The drain on your resources may be strained when only one part-ner has children by a previous marriage. They are more likely to be highly stressed if both of you bring children to the marriage. And you may feel that your resource cupboard is nearly bare if you both have children from your previous marriages plus children from your present marriage.

Donna, for instance, has a son by her first marriage. She mar-ried Tracy, whose first wife had abandoned him and their two chil-dren. Donna and Tracy have had two children since their marriage, giving them a total of five. The children they brought to the mar-riage are seven to ten years older than the children they had togeth-er. Donna points out some of the problems they have encountered:

"When I was a single mother, I spent a lot of time with Keith, my son. When Tracy and I married, I suddenly found myself having to attend to three children instead of one. And now we have five. The time I can give to Keith has changed dramatically. And this bothers me. I don't want him to feel that he's any less important to me just because of the other children.

"Then there are things like birthdays and Christmas. After the divorce, I probably spent more on Keith than I should have. His father rarely saw him, and I tried to make up for the loss by making sure he had everything he wanted. But now neither Keith nor Tracy's two children get as much as they did before we were married and had two more children.

"I don't mind this too much. They get all they need. But I just don't want the older three to feel that we love the other two more than we love them. I also don't want any of them to grow up and feel that they didn't have enough time with us. But until they invent a 48-hour day, I don't think we can give any of them any more than we're giving them right now."

As Donna realized, a "yours, mine, and ours" situation is sensitive not only because of the strain on resources, but also because of the anxiety that the children who were brought into the marriage may have about the children born to the couple. Children with only one natural parent in the home understandably may wonder whether those with both natural parents will be loved more.

HOW TO USE YOUR RESOURCES WISELY

There are a number of things you can do to make the best use of your resources. You can't add to the hours in your day, but you may be able to make better use of them. Even without a substantial increase in your income, you can deal with, or even avoid, the money struggles that occur in stepfamilies. You can expand your social network and hone your spiritual tools, without additional hours in the day or greater financial resources. Here are some specific things you can do:

1) Develop time-management skills. There are a number of basic principles of time management that work well for stepfamilies. They increase efficiency as well as nurture good relationships:

• Make a list of tasks that need to be done by each member of the stepfamily. You will find that just writing them down can alleviate your anxiety because you don't have to juggle countless things in your head. Among other things, a list can help you organize tasks so you are more time-efficient that you accept the fact that low-priority items may or may not get done.

• Prioritize. Prioritizing means that you accept th fact that low-priority items may not get done. It means you don't really have to do everything, only those things which, in your understanding of God's calling, are priority items.

• Set time limits. Parkinson's Law states that work expands to fill the time available for its completion. You need not be rigid about time limits, but if you don't at least have a limit in mind you may find yourself spending far more time than necessary on some tasks. Moreover, like having a list, setting time limits can be very comforting. Deciding that it will take two hours to clean the house if each member does his or her part, for example, is both motivating and comforting to busy people who have to schedule other things.

• Use the Premack principle. This psychological principle states that you should do things in order from the least to the most desirable. Doing the task you dislike the most gets it out of the way. And by doing a more desirable job next, you are, in effect, rewarding yourself for completing the earlier one. Following this principle, therefore, will make you more effective and efficient in doing tasks you dislike.

• Do more than one task at a time whenever possible. As many people have discovered, it is possible to talk on the telephone while cooking, make repairs while watching TV, make plans for the next day while standing in a line, and so forth. There are times when doing two or more things at once will free you to spend more time with your spouse and stepfamily.

• Learn to avoid time traps. There are some common ways to waste time. If you tend to procrastinate, hold to the Premack principle and reward yourself in some way for completing a task. If you are a perfectionist, ask yourself if your time is better spent making the house spotless or spending time with your stepfamily. If you waste time making minor decisions, find a more effective way to decide. For instance, designate someone to decide or take turns making the decision.

• Use all available help for household tasks. "All available help" includes everyone in the stepfamily. Within the limits of your budget, consider taking advantage of such things as a cleaning service, yard-care service, or carry-out meals. We are not saying you should use such services, only that you should consider them if they free up more time for nurturing your stepfamily.

• Ask, "How else could we? . . ." This question directs you to be creative. How else could you do what you're doing so that you have more time or less strain on your budget? Sometimes even a simple change can be highly beneficial. For instance, a wife who was concerned about too little time with her husband offered to go with him when he picked up his daughter on weekends. They found that the drive gave them time to talk—twenty minutes of uninterrupted intimacy that greatly enriched their marriage.

2) Learn to say no. Do you have trouble saying no to people? Does it bother you to turn down an invitation even if you prefer to stay home? Do you find it difficult to tell someone you can't be a helper at church or a volunteer for a worthy cause? Do you feel you must agree to every request from a family or stepfamily member?

Many people have a hard time saying no, even though their schedules are jammed with responsibilities. If you're one of them, you may find it useful to get a good book on assertiveness and learn the skills it advocates. You may also find it useful to remind yourself that God models for us the need to say no at times; as many writers on prayer point out, one of the answers that God gives to our requests is no. Jesus gave a negative answer to the disciples after the resurrection when they asked him if he was going to restore the kingdom: "It is not for you to know times or periods that the Father has set by his own authority" (Acts 1:7).

It is both appropriate and necessary to say no to some requests and some desires. Gregg, a stepfather to an adolescent boy, shares how learning to say no has lead to a satisfying stepfamily life:

> "We don't have as nice a home as some people we know. We don't drive a late-model car. There are times when my stepson wants something that we feel is too expensive. We simply tell him we're sorry, but we can't afford it. We try to suggest alternatives.
>
> "One of the reasons we don't have as much as others is that my wife didn't work during the years my stepson was growing up. In fact, she still only works part-time, so she can be there when he gets home from high school.
>
> "But there's another reason. We simply decided from the start that we were not going to get mired in debt. We both knew from our first marriages that money can be a big issue. We decided that it wouldn't be an issue for us. There are enough struggles in a stepfamily without fighting over money.
>
> "And there's a third reason. Since neither of us works long hours in order to have a higher income, we can give the time we need to our family. And it's really paid off."

Gregg and his wife decided to say no to a higher standard of living. They have said no to demands on their time when they believed those demands would strain their stepfamily relationships. They have said no to their son/stepson when his requests were out of line with their standards. He hasn't always received their no happily. But he is happy about his stepfamily. Gregg and his wife are also happy. A judicious no from time to time has benefitted them enormously.

3) Discuss money values and set up a budget. Don't do one without the other. We suggest you begin with a discussion of money values with your spouse. There are a number of questions you each need to answer: Is one of you more of a spender than the other? What are your financial goals? What did each of you learn about the meaning of money in the homes in which you grew up? How many of those ideas do you still hold?

An interesting way to start your discussion is for each of you to write down all the words you can think of that deal with money. For instance, you might have such things on your list as: nest egg, cushion, vacation, child support, mortgage, the children's education, and so on. Talk about what each of those items mean to you. The lists themselves are an indication of the ways in which each of you value money. Your discussion will clarify the things that are important to each of you as you make up your budget.

Moreover, we strongly recommend a written budget—a budget with which each of you is familiar and to which each of you has agreed. There are good books and computer programs to help you develop such a budget.

As you work out your budget, we suggest that it include, if at all possible, two line items: one discretionary account for you and one for your spouse. Your discretionary account is money that is yours to save or to spend for anything you want—no questions asked. Your discretionary account frees you from feeling constrained every time you see something you would like to buy, and also avoids the common marital argument of overspending.

You will also have to decide whether to have one (ours), two (yours and mine), or three (yours, mine, and ours) checking and saving accounts. Some couples decide that one account has important symbolic meaning for them—it indicates their trust in each other and their commitment to be "one flesh." In some cases, however, one spouse brings a great many debts to the union while the other spouse is relatively debt-free. These couples may decide that two or three accounts work better for them, at least until the debts are paid.

There is no one way of working out a budget that is best. Whatever works for you is what you should do. And be flexible. If you choose an arrangement that doesn't work well, change it.

4) *Don't use money to ease guilt or to purchase love.* Yes, your children were hurt by divorce and this makes you feel guilty. Yes, you desperately want your stepchildren to love you. But no, you can't spend away their hurt and your guilt, and you can't buy your stepchildren's love. Furthermore, as Bonnie, a stepmother, illustrates in the following account, using money to ease guilt or to purchase love is only likely to create other problems:

> "I have three children and a stepson, Brendan. Paul, my husband, felt really guilty about his marriage breaking up. Brendan was seven at the time and he resented Paul for leaving home. Paul's way of dealing with his guilt is to buy Brendan whatever he wants. And Brendan often wants things we can't afford. So now Paul has to deal with my resentment as well as Brendan's.
>
> "Sometimes it gets real crazy, because Paul and his ex start competing with each other. Brendan wanted a new baseball glove. Naturally, he wanted the most expensive one. Paul and I argued about it, but I finally gave in and Paul bought it. Then he found out that his ex bought the glove just before he did, so Brendan didn't need it. Well Paul blamed me, because he would have bought it sooner if I hadn't objected. That led to another argument. We have to put an end to this sort of thing."

Bonnie is right. If they don't put an end to it, it could put an end to their stepfamily.

Using money to deal with hurt and guilt or to purchase love not only fails in its purpose, but it also creates new problems. In addition to her resentment and conflict with Paul, Bonnie is convinced that both Brendan and her own children are learning two things that could damage their futures. First, they are learning how to manipulate others. Bonnie believes that Brendan is aware, and takes advantage, of the competition between his mother and father to please him. She also believes that her own children recognize the way in which Brendan manipulates his parents.

Second, Bonnie fears that the children are learning that it's appropriate to use money as a tool for dealing with interpersonal issues. As she sees it, Brendan and her own three children are not oblivious to the fact that the gifts are an extravagant means to win affection and approval. Bonnie doesn't want the children to grow up thinking they can buy their way into good relationships.

We agree with Bonnie. Paul's indulgence of Brendan is understandable in the sense that he desperately wants to ease Brendan's hurt and keep his affection. But it is, in every way, counterproductive. In addition to the destructive consequences that Bonnie recognizes, Paul's extravagance also uses up resources that could be available for his stepchildren, making it more difficult for them to believe that he cares as much for them as he does for Brendan.

5) Cultivate your social network. We have seen time and again the insights gained, the encouragement found, and the emotional support developed as the result of a strong social network. If you already have a strong social network of relatives and friends who understand and support you, cherish and continue those relationships. If you feel perplexed, isolated, overwhelmed, or otherwise vexed in your efforts to build a satisfying stepfamily life, we urge you to enlarge your social network. In particular, we suggest you join a stepfamily support group at your church or a local chapter of the Stepfamily Association of America.

A common reaction we hear from people who join such groups is, "It helped us so much just to hear that others have faced the same kinds of problems. We listened to them and thought, 'We know exactly what you're talking about because we've struggled with the same thing.'" You are never more alone than when you are caught up in a tumultuous situation that you think is unique to you. When you are part of a group, you realize that your situation isn't unique after all. You are no longer alone in your struggles.

If you live in an area where no support groups are available, you can start one. You can use this book, including the materials in the appendix which are designed for discussion groups. The Stepfamily Association of America also will provide you with excellent materials for group discussions. If you don't want to form a group, at least try to find one or more stepfamilies with whom you can be friends. We won't claim that you can't forge a satisfying stepfamily life without such support, but why try to climb over a wall on your own if someone else is there to offer a hand?

6) *Maintain regular family meetings.* We have pointed out the importance of family meetings a number of times. We suggest that you hold such meetings regularly. They provide excellent forums in which to discuss the various challenges posed by resources: how to make the time needed for stepfamily life, how money should be viewed and handled, how to maintain helpful relationships with others, and how to have a strong spiritual foundation.

To make family meetings effective, they should include various kinds of discussions. In particular, try to include at least some of the following in each meeting:

- discussion of the good things that have happened in your stepfamily since the last meeting

- expressions of appreciation by the parent and stepparent for achievements, help, good behavior, etc., of the children or stepchildren

- discussion of problems or challenges presently facing the stepfamily, with suggestions from each member on how to deal with them

- allocation of household tasks, if necessary, so that each stepfamily member carries some share of the load (it also may be useful to ask if anyone would like to trade a task with someone else)

- discussion of schedules, with brainstorming to help each other be effective in the use of time

- planning for regular, shared stepfamily activities

Family meetings should be more than a time to thrash out problems. You don't want stepfamily members to think of the meetings as nothing more than distasteful confrontations. In addition to addressing problems and concerns, the meetings should also be a time when you affirm each other, build solidarity, plan for things everyone wants to do, and ensure that each member feels that household tasks are fairly distributed.

7) Maintain a strong spiritual focus. We asked a stepmother what she had learned that would be of help to other stepparents. She said:

> "What I'm learning is to give it to God. That's hard. I sometimes tell God, 'I'm trusting you to help me with this,' but I still hang on to the problem and fret about it as though God wasn't involved. But I'm learning. I'm learning that, as I give myself and my stepfamily to God, he gives me hope and joy. I'm not alone in this struggle. God is with me. Other people are there, other people who are going through some of the same things. And the church is there. So I guess I would sum it up by saying to other stepparents, 'Trust in God to help you. Your faith will grow tremendously, and you will be able to work through the problems and experience the joy of a fulfilling life.'"

This stepmother, like many others, has learned about the need for, and the power of, spiritual resources. We asked a group of stepfamily members how Christian resources have helped them deal with the challenges of stepfamily life. Here are some of their responses:

> "We go to church and pray together regularly. We take my stepson to Sunday School. We joined a couples group at the church. We have tried to be faithful to God, and he has blessed us richly. Our stepfamily works well. In fact, it works very well. And that's because we built it on the foundation of our faith in God" (a stepfather with one stepson).

> "Spiritual resources are one of the most important of all our resources. My husband and I both find that we have to continue in Bible study and pray regularly in order to maintain our equi-

librium. When one of my stepsons was having a drug problem, I went through the Spiritual Twelve Steps while he went through a treatment program. I also take advantage of a yearly women's retreat because I know I have to keep myself spiritually strong" (a stepmother with two children and three stepchildren).

"My church has helped me keep focused on holding onto sound family values and maintaining a loving, forgiving environment in our home. Prayer has really helped me when the going gets tough. Prayer takes away the anger and hostility, and replaces it with peace. Worshipping together reminds each of us about the importance of forgiveness and getting along together. It's helped to keep harmony in our family, because it helps us keep our differences in perspective and focus on what's really important in life" (a stepfather with one stepdaughter and two children).

As these statements indicate, spiritual resources are enormously important in dealing with challenges and creating the kind of stepfamily life that is rewarding to each member. In order to draw on spiritual resources, you need to actively and purposefully maintain a strong spiritual focus in your life and the life of your stepfamily. The stepfather who pointed out how prayer enables him to deal with anger and hostility does not confine his prayer life to times when something angers him. Rather, having cultivated his skills through regular prayer, he finds it natural and easy to use this resource when he feels anger and hostility.

Similarly, he does not resort to spiritual resources only when his stepfamily is foundering on the rocks of turmoil and conflict. As with his marriage, he affirms his faith "for better and for worse." That is, he uses his spiritual resources when things are going well and when things are not going well. And the net result is a satisfying stepfamily life.

"You're Not My Father"
The Challenge of Stepparenting

In most cases, stepparenting is the most difficult hurdle you'll face in creating a successful stepfamily. Take 10-year-old Adam and his stepfather, Michael, for instance. Adam's mother, Jennie, married Michael when Adam was three years old. It was Michael's first marriage, and he was committed to being a good father to Adam and to the three children that he and Jennie eventually had together. Although Michael and Adam have developed a close relationship over the years, there have been problems, largely because Michael has resented Adam's father's involvement in Michael's life. According to Michael:

> "In every practical way, I am Adam's father. For most of his life, I have provided the day-to-day care that a child needs from a dad. Adam's biological father, who plays with a rock band and is on the road most of the year, shows up from time to time for a couple of weeks and he upsets everything. He comes on like gangbusters. Adam acts up, I get angry, and our whole family is thrown into turmoil. Every time this happens I begin to feel that Adam is not my child, and I am not his father. I know that I'm important in his life, but I somehow really feel diminished by this stepparent role."

Feeling diminished is only one of a dismal package of negative emotions that stepparents tend to experience. And a problem with a stepchild's biological parent is only one of many irksome challenges that stepparents are likely to face.

Even though we believe that stepparenting is the greatest hurdle of all in the effort to build a satisfying stepfamily life, we want to begin this exploration with a word of encouragement: "In the world you face persecution. But take courage; I have conquered the world!" (John 16:33). Keep this promise of Jesus firmly in mind as you face the challenges of stepparenting.

THE CHALLENGE OF STEPPARENTING

Every stepparent faces four realities that make stepparenting difficult and complex:

1) Stepparents begin with expectations based on fantasy. We noted in chapter 3 that people tend to have expectations based on fantasy about stepfamily life in general. A number of those expectations are attached to the job of stepparenting. For example, how many of the following did you expect when you first became a stepparent?

- gratitude for accepting parental-like responsibilities

- acceptance as an authority figure

- acceptance of you as a family member

- recognition and respect as a caring adult

- willingness of your stepchildren to engage in household chores

- a rapidly growing affection and trust between you and your stepchildren

- a settled, orderly life

Such expectations quickly shatter the realities of stepparenting. Some of these expectations may eventually be realized, but they rarely happen as quickly and easily as people expect. You may be one of the few people blessed with an easy experience, but you are more likely to encounter such things as those expressed by other stepparents:

• "I feel more like a maid than a mother."

• "My stepdaughter never seems to be grateful for anything I do; she certainly never says 'thank you' to me."

• "After two years, I still sometimes feel like an outsider, like my wife and stepchildren are a group that I'll never be part of."

• "My stepson seems to be grading me on everything I do. It's like I have to be Mrs. Perfection twenty-four hours a day or he'll have proof that I'm unfit to be a stepmother."

• "I'm beginning to wonder if my stepson will ever get over his hostility towards me."

• "I feel that, every time I try to set some rules, it's like a declaration of war with my stepchildren."

You are better off to expect resistance and conflict. If you don't experience them, be grateful. If you do, remind yourself that your experience is typical and that God's grace will enable you to deal effectively with the situation.

2) The term "stepparent" has negative connotations to most people. This is particularly true for stepmothers. In fact, your stepchildren have probably read stories about a "wicked" stepmother while growing up. No wonder stepmothers tend to find it more difficult to raise stepchildren than stepfathers do. Who wants a stepmother after hearing those horror stories?

People also react negatively to the terms "stepfather" and "stepchild." Many people believe that stepparents—whether male or female—are less likely to be supportive than biological or adoptive parents. In other words, they believe that stepparents are less likely to be involved with or concerned about their stepchildren. And the children, therefore, are deprived of the intense, loving bond that people expect from a biological parent. Consequently, the stepparent-stepchild relationship may begin with the stepchild expecting to be shortchanged by the relationship.

3) There is no consensus on the stepparent role. Think about your various roles in life: son or daughter, student, worker, spouse. For most of your roles, you don't have to spend time puzzling over how to behave. This is because you grew up in a society where there is a fair amount of consensus on what these roles demand. But what does it mean to be a stepparent? Perhaps, in time, there will be more consensus on the stepparent role. But currently, most people find themselves defining the role by trial and error.

A group of researchers studied forty stepfamilies and found considerable differences about how the role of stepparent is perceived. About half of the parents and stepparents chose the term "parent" to describe the stepparent role. The other half selected the term "stepparent" or "friend" to describe this role. In contrast, the stepchildren preferred "friend" over the other terms to describe their stepparents' role.

Thus, even if you and your spouse agree on what it means to be a stepparent, your stepchildren may have a very different view. If there is disagreement in your stepfamily, you are typical of those who must struggle to create the stepparent-stepchild roles in your stepfamily.

4) You are required to engage in parenting behavior before you are emotionally bonded with the child. Recall that bonding is the process of forming a secure, emotional attachment. Generally, bonding occurs naturally between biological parents and their children. It also begins early—even before the child is born. A few years ago, we gathered over one thousand experiences of joy from people. Not surprisingly, one of the joyous experiences reported by women was holding a newborn child. And one of the joyous experiences noted by men was watching a pregnancy develop and being present at the birth. One father told us how he would caress his wife's abdomen, put his ear to it, and talk softly to his unborn child. Through such experiences, people bond with their children even before they are born.

As a stepparent, you weren't present at the birth of your stepchild. You didn't delight in his first smiles nor feel his total dependence on you for nurture and protection when you held him close. And yet, you now are expected to respond to this child as though you had experienced all of these wonderful things.

Keep in mind, as we pointed out in chapter 3, your goal is to be a stepparent, not a parent nor a super-parent. However, before we provide guidelines for doing this, we want to look at the thorny issue of discipline in stepfamily life.

THE BIG "D": DISCIPLINE

Discipline can be a vexing issue in any family. Most arguments about children are differences about discipline. Based on the experience of other stepfamilies, we offer the following suggestions for dealing with discipline:

1) Decide who will be responsible for discipline. We don't know any parent or stepparent who enjoys disciplining a child. It is tempting, therefore, to let the spouse who finds it least onerous to take over the task. This can be a prelude to disaster. We know a father who turned over all discipline matters to his wife. She was responsible for disciplining both her own children and her stepchildren. "You're the mother in this house," he would say when she entreated him to help with his children. "Make them realize they have to obey you." She never could. And, unfortunately, their marriage didn't make it.

There are various ways to handle the responsibility for discipline, none of which is inherently better than the others. For example, you could each discipline your own children. This is what

Harry and Blanche advocate. They have a solid marriage and a satisfying stepfamily (he had one child and she had two when they
married). Harry says:

> "We each agreed to handle the discipline for our own children.
> We often discuss how to handle a problem, but the parent has the
> final decision. And we never say 'I told you so' if the decision
> doesn't work out.
>
> "You can't come into a marriage with children and start
> changing all the rules and expect total compliance. We decided
> that we could each have some different rules for our children.
> They know that their own parent sets the rules and their own
> parent enforces the rules. So they can't complain if they're treat-
> ed a little differently from each other."

What works for Harry and Blanche may not work for others. In
other stepfamilies, the parent and stepparent work as a team in disciplining. Either arrangement has both advantages and disadvan-
tages. Do what works for you and your stepfamily. You may find
that you need to change the arrangement depending on the situation. You may also change as your relationship with your stepchildren develops or as they grow older; in both cases, you may find it
better to become more involved in the discipline.

2) Be aware of the typical pitfalls of discipline. If you believe any
of the following to be true, you need to have a serious discussion
with your spouse and work out a new and mutually acceptable
arrangement:

• I and/or my spouse believe there is only one correct way to
discipline children.

• My spouse is too harsh in disciplining my child.

• My spouse can't get my child to respect or obey him or her.

• My spouse won't take any responsibility for discipline.

• My spouse is much easier on his or her children than on
mine.

These pitfalls threaten the stability of stepfamily life. For example, a mother of two who married a father of two tells how her stepfamily nearly came apart over the issue of discipline:

"My husband had custody of his two children, and he was very kind and patient with them. I expected him to be the same with mine after we were married. This didn't happen.

"From the first, he acted as if his children never did anything wrong, while mine were always doing something wrong. He yelled at my children and insisted on punishing them, but never saw any reason to discipline his. We fought all the time about the matter. He actually believed that I was too easy on my kids and too hard on his. And I was certain that he was too easy on his and too hard on mine.

"We were about ready to call it quits, but neither of us wanted a second divorce. So we went into counseling. We finally worked out a better way to relate to each other's kids. But I still worry that the children—both my own and my stepchildren—will always suffer from the terrible battles they had with their stepparents and the fierce arguments they heard between my husband and me."

3) Decide on the kind of discipline you will use. As in the case just cited, there may be a disagreement on whether a child needs to be disciplined. Often, however, the disagreement is over how a child should be disciplined.

You have many options. Physical punishment is one. Most experts agree that physical punishment is inappropriate and even damaging for older children. At young ages, before the child has the capacity to reason about a behavior, mild spanking can be effective in some situations.

The "time-out" method is an effective way to discipline young children. The child is required to sit alone and do nothing for a period of time designated by the adult. Loss of privileges also works for many children. Taking away a favorite toy for a time, not allowing a child to engage in a favorite activity, turning the television off, and so on are ways to take away privileges.

Emotional withdrawal is one form of discipline that should never be used. Statements such as, "Mommy won't love you if you do that," or emotional coldness that give the child the same message are counterproductive efforts. They can damage the child and your relationship with him or her.

A different approach, particularly as children reach school age, is to allow them to suffer the natural consequences of their behavior. You may want to explain the consequences in advance where possible. For instance, if a child is responsible for picking up his or her clothes, you may explain that the child will not be able to watch television until the clothes are picked up. The next time the child does not pick up the clothes, the natural consequence is that the television cannot be turned on until the task is done. Similarly, a child who spills milk on the table cloth may be required to clean up the mess rather than being reprimanded or told to leave the table.

This way, children learn to take responsibility for their own behavior. The children learn, "If we do this, or fail to do this, then this is what will happen."

Finally, rewarding desired behavior is another form of discipline. You can punish a child for being late, or you can reward the child for being on time. You can punish a child for not doing homework, or you can reward a child for doing well in school.

Having said all this, we underscore these three points about discipline:

• Discipline is necessary for the child's and the family's well-being; permissiveness is a poor teacher for learning to live in a world of rules.

• There is no single form of discipline that is appropriate for every child; you may have to use different kinds of discipline for the various children in your home.

• There is no single form of discipline that is appropriate for every situation; you may have to discipline the same child in different ways given different situations.

4) Keep in mind that discipline is only one aspect of the job of stepparenting. Stepparents who are involved in disciplining sometimes get caught in the trap of evaluating how well they function as a stepparent solely on the basis of how well the discipline works, or how well they think it works. You need to keep two things in mind. First, no child expresses gratitude for having been disciplined. You and your spouse will need to judge the effectiveness of your methods by evaluating the child's growth and development.

Second, don't evaluate your stepparenting solely on the basis of how well the discipline seems to be working. Discipline is necessary because it teaches children how to function within socially acceptable boundaries of behavior. But you have other important tasks, too. Nurturing, affirming, guiding, and giving affection to your stepchild are as crucial to your stepchild as discipline. As a man said of his stepfather:

> "I remember there were times when I thought he was disciplining me unfairly. I remember thinking to myself that I would never treat my own children that way. But now I can't remember what he did that I thought was unfair or even why he did it. Instead, what I remember is that he really cared about me. I remember the pride in his eyes when I did well at school. I remember the joy on his face when I asked him to participate in my wedding. And I remember the love and gratitude he expressed when I was with him just before he died."

TWELVE PRINCIPLES OF EFFECTIVE STEPPARENTING

There are no easy shortcuts to effective stepparenting; nor will the following principles always be easily practiced. They will require self reminders, self-control, and practice.

1) Stepparenting means involvement, not detachment. This may sound like an unnecessary statement, but we make it the first principle because some stepparents, and particularly stepfathers, adopt a laissez-faire style with their stepchildren. From the stepparent's point of view, the style may be intended to say, "I know I'm not your parent, so I won't try to run your life. You may do as you please. I'm here if you need me, but I won't interfere."

Whatever the stepparent's intent, from the stepchild's point of view a detached stepparent says, "I don't care that much about you. You're not that important in my life." The pioneer American psychologist and philosopher, William James, once observed that the worst possible punishment for a human—worse even than physical abuse—is to be treated as nonexistent. Detachment is a way of doing this—of treating someone else as virtually nonexistent. It is, therefore, a punitive rather than a helpful way of dealing with others.

Nevertheless, you might think that a laissez-faire approach would suit adolescents who typically resist authority and might be especially resistant to that of a stepparent. However, an adolescent is more likely to need, which is different from "want," a stepparent who is strongly involved with him or her, including one who shares in the discipline. It is often best to let the biological parent, with the support of the stepparent, discipline younger children. Some stepparents find this arrangement also works with adolescents. But many discover, particularly if the stepfamily is formed when the stepchildren are adolescents, that a high degree of stepparent involvement, including involvement in discipline, works best. Your stepchildren might not appreciate your involvement in the short run, but in the long run they will benefit far more from your involvement than from your detachment.

2) Begin by being a friend to your stepchildren. Unless your stepchildren are infants, you should begin by befriending them. Make it clear that you have no agenda beyond being good friends with them. Your relationship may develop beyond this. However, it is less likely to do so and more likely to involve conflict if you don't begin simply as friends. Here are some testimonies from stepparents who began as friends and eventually became more like parents than stepparents:

"We realized that you use first names for friends. So we told the stepchildren to call us and their stepsiblings whatever was comfortable for them. At first, our children would introduce their stepsiblings as 'this is my stepbrother' or 'this is my stepsister.' As time went by, the 'step' was gradually dropped, and they simply started identifying each other as brother and sister.

"My wife and I felt a little uncomfortable being called by our first names. But we got used to it. My stepson has always called me by my first name. My three children began by calling my wife by her first name. But now I hear them sometimes call her 'mom,' and I know that's the way they feel about her" (father with three children and one stepson).

"At the beginning, I made it clear to my stepchildren that I didn't want to be their father, only their friend. I tried to nurture my stepson as much as I could. He likes to hunt and fish and so do I, so we spent a lot of time together doing those things. It was harder with my stepdaughter. I think she resented me more than my stepson did. But I took the same approach with her, and we have a good relationship now. I'll go as far with them as they want to go in this relationship, but no farther. They know that, and they've responded positively" (stepfather of two).

"When my mother and father divorced, I lived with my mother. She remarried. From my point of view, it was more important for my stepfather to be a friend to me, not a father. I already had a father, even though I didn't live with him. When my stepfather tried to be my father, I resented him and I was open about my resentment. I never really loved him or felt any affection for him, mainly because I felt he was competing with my father for my affection. So I was cordial, but never affectionate.

"When I became a stepmother, I concentrated on being a friend to my stepson rather than a mother. We have a really good relationship. I feel affection for him, and he seems to feel increasing affection and respect for me. Thankfully, I learned how not to do it from my stepfather and how to do it by remembering how I felt when I got a stepparent" (stepdaughter and mother of a stepson and a son).

*3) **Let your relationship proceed at your stepchildren's pace.*** In the cases above, the relationships that began with friendship gradually grew into more than friendship. If you want similar results, you must let the relationship proceed at the child's pace. You can't force a child to move quickly from friendship to a more familial relationship.

Once you are friends, you can develop a basic trust in each other. Through shared experiences of various kinds, mutual affection grows. As the child recognizes that you are fulfilling various parental functions—nurturing, protecting, and providing—the child will increasingly develop feelings for you that he or she has for a parent. But all of this must take place at the child's pace, which will probably be slower than the pace you would prefer. Be patient and the eventual outcome will be a rewarding one.

*4) **Plan special times and experiences with your stepchildren.*** You are trying to develop an intimate relationship with your stepchildren. Shared experiences, including special occasions, are one way to build intimacy. When you share an experience with your stepchildren, you learn more about each other and build a relational history. When you plan something special for your stepchildren, you send them the message that you care about them and you want them to enjoy life. These are central elements in creating an intimate relationship.

It is important for you and your stepchild to have time alone together. It is also important on these occasions to do something that your stepchild considers special. As a stepmother discovered, this isn't always easy, but it can be done:

> "My stepdaughter and I are very different. I'm an outdoor person. I like to hike, camp out, swim, play tennis—anything outside. My stepdaughter is more like the stereotype of a female. She loves to shop. She loves to read. I don't particularly enjoy either of those things. I knew I needed to do some things with her, but what? If I went shopping just to build our relationship, it could backfire if she realized how miserable I was.

"Fortunately, we both like movies. So we started going to movies together. Just the two of us. After the movie, we would go to a coffee shop, get a couple hot chocolates, and talk about the movie. We grew closer because we had something special together that she didn't even have with her father."

5) *You and your spouse should present a united front to the stepchildren.* The only thing that is harder than raising your children is raising someone else's children. And the job is doubly difficult if you and your spouse don't work as a team, presenting a united front to the children. As one weary stepmother put it:

> "I'm exhausted. Not only do my stepchildren blame me for breaking up their home, but they view me as an ogre because I set rules and try to enforce them. My husband only makes the situation worse, because he is so guilty about his divorce that he gives in to them all the time. He won't back me up if I try to discipline them, and he won't help me put any boundaries on their behavior. I'm not sure I can keep on much longer."

One reason for presenting a united front is that it carries more weight with the children and limits the possibility of them playing one of you against the other. Another reason is that you will be more creative and effective when you work as a team because you will incorporate your individual strengths into your parenting/stepparenting. Moira, a trained counselor, is the mother of one and a stepmother of three. She recognizes the value of both her and her husband's skills as they discipline their four children:

> "We're still working out how to deal with discipline. We have a lot of discussions about it. We work better as a team. When we do, we tend to come up with firm, fair, and appropriate measures. I get angry sometimes when I see my husband try to discipline on his own because he is inconsistent and the kids know it. They take advantage of him. He also rescues them sometimes from the natural consequences of their behavior, and I think that's a mistake.

"I tend to be consistent because of my training. But I know I can be inflexible. That's why we're better as a team. I recommend this approach to other couples. Make it a point to talk together about what you are going to do, even if it means the kids have to wait a little to see how they're going to be disciplined."

As you work as a team, you can draw on each other's strengths and neutralize each other's weaknesses. As you present a united front to the stepchildren, you send the message that neither of you will negate the decision of the other. You also show them that you are truly a couple.

6) Give your stepchildren the gift of limits. As Moira pointed out, you need to "be firm with both your children and your stepchildren. They actually like knowing there are boundaries." Of course, they won't usually let you know that. Nevertheless, it's true. Children do not develop well in a home that is too permissive. They need to know there are limits—boundaries which cannot be crossed without some kind of adverse consequences. If they don't learn the lesson at home, it will be harder for them to learn it as they grow up and try to function outside the home. The limits may be of various kinds:

• unacceptable behavior, such as hitting others

• unacceptable ways of talking, such as calling others names

• limits, as determined by the parent and stepparent, on the amount of money that can be spent on the child/stepchild

• a regular bedtime, which is only changed for special occasions

• a curfew for adolescents

• eating dinner together

As you may have already recognized, limits help establish your stepfamily identity in addition to providing your stepchildren with an ordered environment. That's why we call them a "gift." They contribute to the healthy development of your stepchildren.

7) Use clear and explicit rules to establish limits. You can't expect a child to stay within ill-defined limits. "No one ever told me that" may be a legitimate objection when a child is disciplined for crossing a boundary. From your stepchildren's point of view, rules are clear and explicit when they are:

- consistent with each other

- associated with positive and negative consequences

- stated and explained

- consistently enforced

Be careful to establish consequences that you can reasonably administer. For example, a teen-age girl shared this experience:

> "My stepfather set a time for me to be home from my dates. He also said that I would be grounded for two weeks for every minute I was late. Well, one night my friends and I were having a blast and I completely forgot the time. When I got home, he was waiting up for me. At two weeks per minute, I was grounded for nearly six years!"

Of course, this was unrealistic, and the stepfather had to relent. There should be adverse consequences when rules are broken, but they need to be realistic consequences.

There's one more point to consider: don't overwhelm your stepchildren with a massive number of rules. When setting up rules, ask whether each rule is really needed and the extent to which you can or cannot be flexible. For instance, a stepson recalls an incident when he was a teenager:

> "During the summer months, it was my job to take care of the yard and I was supposed to do it every Thursday. One summer, when I was about fourteen, my birthday fell on Thursday. I wanted to celebrate the day and do things with my friends. But my stepfather refused to let me do anything until I had first taken care of the yard. It took me most of the morning to do the work, and I still remember how oppressed and abused I felt."

The stepfather thought he was teaching his stepson responsibility and the importance of "work before play." The stepson believed he was learning how bull-headed and unfair his stepfather was.

Rules are necessary. But the purpose of rules is to establish a moral order, not to rigidly channel behavior.

8) *Let your stepchildren participate in making the rules.* A family meeting is a good place to formulate and to explicitly state rules. This gives everyone, including your stepchildren, a voice in what is decided. A basic social psychological principle is that people who participate in the decision-making process are far more likely to abide by the decision than those who have a decision imposed on them. Even if the decision isn't what they prefer, people are still more likely to abide by it when they have participated in the process.

Participation doesn't mean the stepchildren should necessarily have the final say in which rules are to be observed. But the process must not be a sham either. The opinions of your stepchildren should be carefully considered and, at times, they should be followed. The stepdaughter who was theoretically grounded for nearly six years, for example, would have asked for a more realistic sanction for lateness. She was not opposed to the idea of a curfew or to sanctions for breaking the curfew. Yet she rightly regarded a six-year grounding as too severe. And the stepson who had to do the yard work on his birthday would have suggested flexibility in the Thursday rule.

We recognize that this is not the most efficient way to establish stepfamily rules. It takes less time for the two adults to simply formulate and announce them. But that is also much less effective. Your children and stepchildren will greatly appreciate having a say, knowing that you respect their opinion and that you care enough about them to want them to live comfortably with the rules of the house.

9) *Be open about your feelings with your stepchildren and encourage them to be open about theirs.* "You're not my father. I hate you." It's a devastating thing to hear. How should the stepfather respond? In one scenario, the stepfather says nothing. But the mother, who is present, immediately shouts at the child, "Don't ever say anything like that. He's the only father you have, and you will respect him." In another scenario, the stepfather angrily responds with similar words. In a third scenario, the stepfather reacts caustically, "Well, I don't much like you either. But I guess we're stuck with each other."

Each of the above responses is a way of discouraging the expression of negative emotions and, at the same time, of deepening the alienation between stepchild and stepparent.

In order to develop an intimate relationship with your stepchildren, you need to create an environment of openness. For example, if your stepchild said, "I hate you," you could respond this way: "I'm sorry to hear that, because I really want us to be friends. Help me understand why you feel this way." Such a response is not only an invitation to engage in a healing process, but also tells the child that it's okay to express feelings openly because they will be dealt with in a rational, accepting manner.

You'll need a good dose of grace to do this. You'll need to practice your second-mile stamina. Your stepchild may put you to the test many times before responding to your efforts in a more positive way. Going the second mile doesn't mean allowing your stepchild to verbally abuse you. But even when you point out that the stepchild has exceeded acceptable limits, try to state the matter in a way that doesn't play on guilt. For instance, don't say, "You really hurt me when you say things like that. I've tried to do my best, and you just treat me like dirt." Instead say, "When you talk like that to someone, it's very hurtful. I don't want you to talk like that to anyone, including me. If you're angry, let's talk about it without saying hurtful things to each other."

10) Use humor. Humor helps you keep your perspective. If you can still laugh about your struggles, they haven't overwhelmed you. Humor helps build a good relationship because people who laugh together enjoy being together. And it can help you maintain the rules, because humor sometimes works when repeated cajoling fails.

A stepmother offers an example of using humor to maintain the rules:

"My adolescent stepson and I get along quite well in general. But he bugged me to no end with his habit of throwing his dirty clothes on his bedroom floor or on the living room couch. My husband and I both told him this was not to be done in our house. Every time we reminded him, he picked them up. But within a day or two, there they were again.

"It was turning into a real struggle between the two of us. At least, it was for me. I reasoned with him, nagged him, and pleaded with him. He was always agreeable, but he kept throwing the clothes around anyway. I wondered whether this was his way of telling me that he didn't really have to live by my standards.

"My husband and I talked about it, and we decided that perhaps I was taking it too personally. After all, every teenager does such things. Still, it bothered me, even if it wasn't directed against me personally. So how should I deal with it?

"I decided to turn it into a game, and have a little fun with it. I made up a letterhead with a chiropractor's name at the top and wrote a letter to myself. The letter was a bill for $250 and a note that said to stop picking up dirty clothes so that my back could get the needed rest. I left the letter open where I knew my stepson would see it.

"Believe it or not, it worked. He was concerned at first, then laughed when he realized that I had done it myself as a joke. But he's rarely thrown any dirty clothes on the floor or couch since then. And we continue to joke about my 'bad back.'"

Using humor to solve a problem isn't always appropriate. But when it is, it's a powerful tool. Don't neglect it. And use it to create fun times with your stepchildren as well as to solve problems. The more fun you have together, the more stable and satisfying your relationship is likely to be.

11) Accept both your responsibility and your limits. What if you have tried to be a friend and your relationship with your stepchild is still not where you would like it to be? Then you must accept both your responsibility and your limits. Your responsibility is to be a stepparent and to engage in the kinds of behaviors we have discussed in this chapter. Moreover, this responsibility doesn't end if your stepchild stubbornly persists in resisting your efforts.

We once read an article by a man who had a Quaker friend with whom he left work every day. They always stopped at the newsstand where the Quaker asked for the daily paper, paid for it, then politely thanked the surly vendor. One day the man asked his friend why he always thanked the vendor. The man pointed out to the Quaker that the vendor didn't seem to appreciate either his business or his kindness. The Quaker's response was straightforward, "Why should I let him determine how I will act?"

The Quaker was living out his Christian faith independently of how others treated him. His behavior did not depend upon the other person's behavior but rather on his understanding of the Christian calling. Recall that Jesus once healed ten lepers even though only one of them was thoughtful enough to return and thank him (Luke 17:11-19). His response to their plea for healing did not depend upon their subsequent expressions of gratitude.

Your calling is to be a stepparent. You are called to engage in stepparenting behavior, even if your stepchild does not respond as you hope. In most cases, you will eventually forge a satisfying relationship if you continue to be responsible. Yet even if that never happens, you are still responsible to live out your calling.

While you are waiting for a satisfying relationship to develop, remind yourself of your limits. Your "limits" mean that you are not God. You cannot shape your stepchild's life to conform to your own image of what it should be. What you can do is focus on your own behavior and make sure that you engage in responsible stepparenting. Above all, entrust the relationship to the Lord who has promised you to be of good cheer because he has overcome the world.

12) Practice gratitude. "Give thanks in all circumstances . . ." (1 Thessalonians 5:18). This directive was written to people who were being persecuted for their faith. It's tough to be grateful when you're suffering. But it can be done. Corrie Ten Boom, the saintly

Christian who helped save Jews from the Nazis during World War II, told about her experience in a flea-infested concentration camp. She and her sister, Betsie, recalled the directive from 1 Thessalonians and decided to try to find something for which to give God thanks. Betsie, however, insisted that they should give God thanks for everything, trusting God to somehow use all things for their good. They even gave thanks for the fleas. Only later did they realize that the fleas kept the German guards out of their barracks and enabled them to have nightly worship services.

We suggest that you learn to practice gratitude. Keep a gratitude journal in which you write down the blessings of each day. Share at least some of your entries at the dinner table or at your family meeting. This will help other stepfamily members to think about things for which they also can be grateful. As you will discover, it's hard to feel both grateful and hostile, both grateful and resentful, both grateful and deprived. It isn't that gratitude is a cure-all for every negative emotion, but gratitude will help you focus on the way in which God is at work, according to his promise to use all circumstances for your well-being. And if you see your stepfamily life as the handiwork of God, you are well on your way to achieving your goal of a gratifying stepparent-stepchild relationship.

Becoming One Flesh
in the Midst of Turmoil
The Challenge of Marital Intimacy

Betty, an apparently troubled stepmother, told us that she and her husband had done a good job with her two stepchildren. They were in their late teens and seemed to be functioning well. "But," she admitted, "our marriage is a disaster." They had put all of their energies into attending to the needs of her stepchildren. Now both children were in college, and they were left alone with each other. Betty said, "This means that we are left with virtually nothing."

The most important challenge facing spouses in a stepfamily is building a strong and vital marriage. Obviously, this is a critical task if the intimacy needs of both partners are to be met. But it is also essential to the health of your stepfamily.

Was Betty correct? Had she and her husband reared two healthy children, but sacrificed their marriage? Only time will tell, but we have our doubts. Children who grow up in a home—whether in a stepfamily or a biological family—where there is not a good marriage are more likely to suffer adverse consequences than are those who grow up in a home with a solid, happy marriage.

A STRONG MARRIAGE: THE FOUNDATION FOR A STRONG STEPFAMILY

We don't believe it's impossible to have a strong stepfamily and to do a good job of parenting and stepparenting children when your marriage is fragile. But we do maintain that your chances of building a stable and satisfying stepfamily are far better if you also build a stable and satisfying marriage. We have worked with many married couples whose difficulties are rooted in the lingering effects of growing up in homes with troubled marriages. A good marriage won't ensure that your stepchildren will be trouble-free in their own intimate relationships (after all, they are already the victims of one disrupted marriage). It will, however, make it more likely that they will have the model and the resources they need to establish meaningful and lasting intimate relationships of their own.

What does it mean to have a strong marriage? Basically, it means that your marriage is both stable and satisfying to you and your spouse. This is more likely to be true if the following are also true for you:

1) You and your spouse are best friends. Some years ago, we did research on more than 300 couples who had been married for fourteen years or longer. Most were first marriages for both spouses, but about two dozen were second marriages for one or both. We wanted to know why their marriages lasted in the face of high divorce rates. The most frequent reason given by both husbands and wives (they were interviewed separately) for their stable and satisfying marriage was "we are best friends."

To say that your spouse is your best friend is to say that you are in an intimate relationship with someone you like and enjoy. As one of the wives said of her husband, "I would want him as a friend even if I weren't married to him."

2) You and your spouse are committed both to marriage and to each other. What does it mean to be committed? For those in stable marriages, the commitment is both to marriage and to the spouse. Commitment to marriage means that you believe in the institution of marriage and in the fact that marriage is a sacred calling from God. As such, it is to be honored, cherished, and enjoyed.

Commitment to your spouse, on the other hand, means that you are committed to facing and working through difficult times so that you protect your spouse's well-being. If you are truly committed to your spouse, you won't allow your spouse to endure long periods of unhappiness in which vexing problems are left unattended because of other demands or interests.

As Betty, the stepmother quoted at the beginning of this chapter, illustrates, stepparenting can consume you. In their commitment to their stepchildren, she and her husband had neglected their commitment to each other. Undoubtedly, there are days and perhaps seasons when every parent and stepparent believes that the time and energies consumed by the children mean that nothing is left for their marriage.

Indeed, there may be brief periods when this is necessary. A stepmother in a "yours, mine, and ours" family told us that, during the few months when their newborn baby was critically ill their marriage took a back seat to the kids. A marriage can survive such experiences. In fact, their devotion to the children during this difficult period "actually bonded them closer, because they all agreed that it was the only thing they could or wanted to do."

Even apart from such crises, there will probably be times when your children and stepchildren get a larger share of your attention than does your marital relationship. If you are committed to your spouse, however, you won't allow this to continue for any extended period of time.

3) *You and your spouse's needs for affection and sex are fulfilled.* If you are good friends, you are already giving each other a certain amount of affection. But if you're like most of us, it's probably not enough. For example, you and your spouse both need:

- physical contact that is warm but nonsexual (one man said he cherishes those occasions when his wife comes up behind him and kisses him on the back of his neck)

- verbal affirmations of love and affection

- nonverbal expressions of affection, such as a warm smile.

- a satisfying sex life

If expressions of affection are an everyday occurrence around your home, you probably also have a good sex life. A stepmother told us that she and her husband display a great deal of physical affection for each other—everything from holding hands when they walk to hugging and kissing regularly—and that their sexual relationship is a natural outgrowth of this affection. "I couldn't turn on sexually," she admitted, "if the only time he touched me or kissed me was when he wanted sex."

Two additional points are important about sex. First, sexual needs vary greatly. Therefore, you should judge the extent to which your needs are fulfilled by your own feelings and not by what you read is the average for couples your age. Second, sexual fulfillment is not as crucial to a good marriage as other matters. Among the 300 couples in our study of long-term marriages, sexual patterns varied widely and not everyone who had a good marriage had an ideal sex life. One woman, in her second marriage, told us that her husband had a disability that prevented them from having sex at all. In her first marriage, she had great sex. But she would choose the second over the first without a moment's thought "because nothing else was good about the first marriage, while everything else is good about the second."

4) *You and your spouse feel good about the way you communicate.* Good communication means that you each share your thoughts, concerns, feelings, and even trivial observations such as the weather with the other. Of course, no one shares everything. You don't tell your spouse every passing thought that comes into your mind. You don't burden your spouse with every transient feeling you experience. So how much is enough? We have two principles that we advocate—principles that are practiced by people in strong, lasting marriages:

- Communicate effectively so you don't force each other to make assumptions. For example, consider the husband who is obviously in an irritable mood but who won't say why or even admit that he is irritable. Perhaps he had a bad day at work. Perhaps he is frustrated with his stepchildren. Perhaps he looked at himself in the mirror and was startled by the aging process. Perhaps he backed into a post and dented the car. Yet he doesn't tell her what has gone wrong. Instead, he forces his wife to make an assumption: "He must be angry with me." She asks herself, "What have I done?" "Nothing," she defensively replies. And the situation goes downhill from there.

- Communicate your daily experiences well so your spouse doesn't feel cut off from any part of your life. Take, for instance, the experience of a couple with whom we worked. The man (H) is a lawyer. His wife (S) stays at home to care for the stepchildren. This is an exchange they had when discussing their situation with us:

S: "You never tell me anything about your work."
H: "I don't want to burden you with my problems."
S: "I don't think of it as a burden. I need to know what goes on at your work. I feel shut out."
H: "I've always believed that you should leave your work problems at the office and not bring them home."

We pointed out two things to the man. First, no one leaves their problems at work. They affect your feelings, and you bring these feelings home with you. Second, his wife was literally pleading with him to open up this part of his life to her. She wants to know something about the struggles he has at work.

Some people may not want to know details about their spouse's work life. That's why we say the important thing is to "feel good" about the way you communicate with each other. Only the two of you can know how much and what kind is enough.

5) *You and your spouse feel good about the way you handle your differences.* This is crucial. If you communicate well, you are also more likely to handle your differences well. There are some wrong ways to argue, but no single right way. Again, the important thing is that you both feel good about the way you handle conflict.

For example, let's say that you differ on the way to discipline your stepson who frequently hits his sister. You think the most effective discipline would be to put him on time-out, but your spouse thinks spanking would be more productive. A wrong way to argue would be for each of you to defend your position and attack the other's without ever reaching a satisfactory conclusion or argue until one of you gives in from fatigue. The tendency, when you argue in this fashion, is to begin attacking each other.

A better way to handle differences is to treat them as problems to be solved jointly. As we tell people in marriage enrichment groups, always confront conflict with "we have a problem" rather than "you are a problem." In the problem-solving approach, you first make sure you agree on the problem (in the above case, the stepson's aggression). Make sure you each know how the other feels about the problem (perhaps one of you feels it is more serious than the other, for example). Then come up with as many possible solutions as you can.

Frequently, people begin with an either-or notion: we have to do this either your way or my way. But there are rarely only two solutions to a problem. And usually you can find a solution that incorporates both of your ideas. In the above case, for example, the couple may decide to go with the more lenient punishment first (the time-out), warning the stepson that the next time the punishment will be more severe.

STEPFAMILY CHALLENGES TO A STRONG MARRIAGE

Incorporating the five principles of a strong marriage into your own marriage may be more difficult for you than for couples in a biological family situation. In particular, the following factors, most of which we have discussed in previous chapters, may turn the path to marital intimacy into a rocky road:

1) The sheer number of time and energy demands in a stepfamily. As Betty, the stepmother quoted at the beginning of this chapter, discovered, you can find yourself so wrung out by the demands of stepparenting that you forget about nurturing your marriage:

> "It isn't that we didn't feel the need to work on our marriage. It just never happened. There was always something that needed to be done with my stepchildren. Or else the problems we had with them didn't leave us with any energy to think about our marriage. There were nights when I fell into bed not wanting to think about anything, not even about getting up the next morning. And the price we paid is a marriage in serious trouble. We have the time to work on it now, but I don't know if we have the energy or the desire."

2) The manipulative skills of children. Children are resourceful and clever in finding opportunities to play one parent against another for their own advantage. This can create havoc in any family and can be a disaster in a stepfamily. If a child can get his or her natural parent to team up against the stepparent, the damage has begun. And if the behavior continues and the parent and stepparent don't recoup their solidarity, the damage may be irreversible.

Incidentally, don't think that you are immune from this if you and your stepchildren have a good relationship. The point of the manipulation may not be to break up your marriage (although some stepchildren have done this), but to gain some advantage. For example, a stepson might complain to his mother that his stepfather is "mean" because he won't let him buy the new toy he wants. The point is not to create disruption in the marriage but simply to get the toy. If the mother plays into the effort and accepts the child's evaluation that her husband has been "mean," she may find herself embroiled in conflict with her husband, however.

3) Loyalty conflicts. Your determination to ensure that your children know you love them can adversely affect your marital relationship. Recall that in chapter 4 we told about Jack and Stephanie and the problem Stephanie had with Jack's open expression of his passion for her because of the reaction of her stepchildren. Often spouses relate differently to each other when their children or stepchildren are around. They may not even be aware of the difference. Yet it happens frequently. We hear such things as:

> "She's very affectionate except when her kids are around. Then she's stand-offish, and it really bothers me."

> "We had plans for the day for just the two of us. Then his daughter called and talked so long that it was too late for us to go."

> "No matter what we're doing or talking about, if her son wants her attention, he gets it. Whatever happened to telling children that it's not okay to interrupt adults whenever they want to?"

4) Fantasy expectations. "We're not going into this blindly," a man about to become a stepfather said. "We know that our biggest challenge is going to be the stepparenting." He was right, of course. Nevertheless, he was about to carry a fantasy expectation into his stepfamily—that the love he and his future wife had for each other would ensure a fulfilling marriage as long as they met the stepparenting challenges.

You can't take your marriage for granted. You can't assume that it will flourish as long as you are able to deal with the challenges of stepparenting. Second marriages, like first marriages, wither and die from neglect.

NURTURING YOUR MARRIAGE

Many couples point out that they could not have survived the step-family experience without a strong marriage. They needed to work as a team, to aid and to support each other, in order to deal with the many challenges of stepfamily life. Some of the ways that you can build a strong marriage are:

1) Nurture your friendship. A friend is someone you like, someone you enjoy being around, someone with whom you want to do things. To say that your spouse is your best friend means that, of all the people you know, this is the person you like best, most want to be around, and with whom you particularly want to share experiences.

If you do not regard your spouse as your best friend, it doesn't mean your marriage won't last. But in the strongest and most satisfying unions, the spouses usually come to think of each other as best friends even if they don't begin that way.

How can you nurture your friendship so that you become and remain best friends? One way is to be good listeners and confidants. In a strong marriage, each spouse listens carefully to the other, tries to understand and support the other, and in turn, regularly confides in the other, who is also a careful listener. To listen means you care about the other person. To confide means you trust and need the other person. Thus, a good indication of the health of a marriage is the extent to which the partners listen to, and confide in, each other.

A second way to nurture friendship is to continue to find things that you enjoy doing together. We advise couples in marriage enrichment groups to regularly plan to do something new together. "Regularly" can mean once a month, once a quarter, twice a year, or whatever works for you. You can do something completely novel for both of you or something that one of you has done or both of you have done separately. The rule is that you have not done it together. You can plan the activity together or take turns being responsible for the planning. Some of the things that couples have planned include:

- hiking a particular trail

- playing golf

- attending an opera

- enrolling in an adult education class at a community college

- taking ballroom dancing instructions

- spending a vacation on a dude ranch

- celebrating the marriage by spending a night at a motel away from the rest of the stepfamily

The possibilities are endless. Occasionally, you might want to include the stepchildren or another couple in your activity. But most of the time it should involve just the two of you. You may not enjoy everything you do; however, it will be an adventure to anticipate and try something new together on a regular basis. You will discover some things you really enjoy doing together.

A third way to nurture friendship is to cultivate those qualities your spouse appreciates and admires in others. Friends like each other. They appreciate and admire certain qualities in each other. When you cultivate the qualities that your spouse admires in other people, you are nurturing your friendship.

Obviously, you can't cultivate everything your spouse appreciates and admires. But there are certain qualities that virtually everyone appreciates and that everyone can cultivate: sensitivity, kindness, patience, warmth, and so on. A husband who said he and his wife were best friends shared this example of how he had deliberately cultivated a quality his wife admired:

"My wife's father is a self-centered man. He is very concerned about anything that affects his needs but very thoughtless about anyone else's needs. When we visit him, he never asks about us, our jobs, or our stepfamily. He just talks about his own needs.

"Growing up with such a father, my wife developed a real admiration for men who are sensitive and thoughtful about the needs of others. Once, when I had been insensitive to her, she angrily told me that she needed a husband who really cared about her and about other people.

"I took that to heart, and began to work on myself. I had to remind myself when I was in various situations that I was there to care about other people and their needs. Not to focus on my own. It wasn't easy. I still find myself sometimes thinking about how I look in a particular situation rather than how I'm responding to other people's needs. But now I'm a lot more sensitive to my wife and to others than I was in the past."

This husband cultivated sensitivity in direct response to his wife's need and admiration for this quality. And it has been one of the factors that has enhanced their friendship and strengthened their marriage.

2) Avoid triangulation. "Triangulation" is the term family therapists use to describe coalitions within the family. A parent and child can form a coalition against the stepparent. Stepchildren can form a coalition against the parent and stepparent. A parent and stepparent can form a coalition against a child/stepchild. A parent and child can form a coalition against a stepparent and a stepsibling. As with so many other facets of family life, the possibilities for triangulation in a stepfamily are even more extensive and complex than are those in a biological family. Yet whatever the coalition, it is a peril to the well-being and stability of the stepfamily.

Martha and Stewart found themselves confronting the threat of triangulation when they brought their two sets of children together. Martha was a widow with three children. Stewart was divorced, but had custody of his two children. Martha's three children were thirteen, eleven, and nine years of age. Stewart's two children were twelve and nine. The two nine-year-olds were both boys. The trouble, as Martha notes, began with the nine-year-olds:

"They had both been the baby and used to getting a lot of attention. Now they had to share that position. Worse, they had to share a bedroom. We didn't realize how much they disliked and competed with each other at first. Before long, the two babies rallied their own siblings to their respective sides in the struggle. And it was my children against Stewart's children.

"We almost had a disaster. The children started shouting at each other and shoving each other one evening. I thought my kids were the innocent victims, and Stewart believed that his were innocent. And so Stewart and I also got caught up in the battle. Fortunately, Stewart had the presence of mind to call for a time out while he and I discussed what was happening.

"We agreed that we had to stick together, that even natural brothers and sisters get into fights, and that we would firmly insist that the children deal with their differences in a better way. We got through that night and the next. And eventually the children got to be pretty good friends with each other, with the exception of the two babies. They are now nineteen, and still have little use for each other. Their relationship hurts us, but we've survived it because Stewart and I wouldn't allow our family to degenerate into warring camps."

Clearly, their marriage as well as their stepfamily could have become the victim of "warring camps." They have not yet been able to reconcile the two youngest to each other, but neither have they allowed their sons' hostility to draw other stepfamily members into coalitions.

The most common form of triangulation in stepfamilies is probably that of child and parent against stepparent. A stepson recalls how he knowingly worked to pit his mother against his stepfather:

"Most of the time, I got along pretty well with my stepfather. But I always thought he was too hard on me. And I always let my mother know about it. I remember one time when I was pretty young he spanked me on my leg. It was red where he hit me. My mother wasn't around at the time, so I kept hitting the place myself to keep it red until my mother got home. Then I ran to her crying and showed her the spot. This caused an argument between them.

"I also thought my stepfather was stingy. I could always count on him to say no when I wanted something. So I learned to go to my mother. And she would usually—not always, but usually—respond to my distress by buying me whatever I wanted. Well, that caused some arguments too.

"How do I feel about it now? I'm certainly not proud of what I did. I know I caused a lot of strife in our home. I'm happy to say that it didn't break up the marriage. And after I left home, I think their marriage was better than ever."

Your marriage can survive triangulation. But it will be far more stable and satisfying if you don't allow the triangulation to occur in the first place.

3) *Control what you say about your stepchildren.* There is "a time to keep silence, and a time to speak" (Ecclesiastes 3:7). Happy is the stepparent who knows the difference. It's the kind of thing you learn from trial and error, and from discussing the matter with your spouse. As Suzanne, a young woman about to become a stepmother, said to us:

> "I'm just not sure what to do about his daughter. She'll live with us. She and I have a really good relationship so far. She talks to me a lot and even asks my advice about things. But I'm not sure what to do when she misbehaves. Right now, I go to my fiancee whenever I see her doing something or I hear her say something that I think is inappropriate. He thinks I shouldn't do that, that I should just tell her myself, that she respects me enough that she'll listen to what I say. But I don't want to spoil my relationship with her, and I don't want this to be an issue in our marriage."

Her fiancèe responded:

"I don't want my daughter to think that Suzanne tattles on her. I believe that this will be more damaging to their relationship than if Suzanne just tells my daughter whenever she is out of line."

We pointed out that they were approaching the issue in the proper way by discussing it with each other and by recognizing the perils involved. The stepdaughter may change after the marriage. Or she may begin to resist once Suzanne regularly tries to correct her. And she may try to pit her father against Suzanne to get what she wants. Fortunately, Suzanne and her fiancee are aware of all these possibilities and are discussing the best way to deal with the situation.

Whatever they decide, however, they may still have to use trial and error to find the best solution. As a veteran stepmother told us in response to our question about the greatest challenge to the happiness and stability of her stepfamily:

"There are a number. But I think the greatest has been my husband's strong love and loyalty to his children. They were teenagers and he had custody of them when we married. I didn't always agree with his methods of dealing with them. But it's not like they were my children. I didn't have the same right as a mother to say how they should be raised. Early on, when I did say something, it only led to an argument and hurt feelings.

"So I realized that the best thing for me to do when I thought he was overindulging them was to keep my mouth closed. Learning to keep quiet is a major lesson for a stepparent. Sometimes you just have to turn your back on something that rankles you.

"It's also been a challenge to me to keep quiet about my opinion of my stepchildren's mother. I think she's really treated them badly. But I never say anything against her, no matter what she does. I did it once. Only once. I learned from their reaction never to do it again."

This stepmother has a good relationship with her stepchildren and a strong marriage. As she acknowledges, those rewards are due in no small measure to learning when to speak and when to maintain silence.

4) *Whenever possible, take preventive action.* To take preventive action requires that you do what is necessary and practical to avoid problems or to deal with them before they become more serious. You can avoid a certain number of problems simply by reading books or participating in a stepfamily support groups or talking to other stepparents. From such sources, you learn some of the typical problems that occur in stepfamilies. Knowing what they are in advance, you can often take steps to avoid them.

For example, you know that problems typically arise over what a stepchild will call the stepparent. And you know that you can escalate the problem by insisting that your stepchild call you Mom or Dad. It's easy to avoid the problem by simply allowing the stepchild to call you whatever he or she prefers.

You can't always anticipate a problem. But it is usually possible to prevent it from looming large and threatening your marriage and your stepfamily by taking action to deal with it in the early stages. The necessary preventive action may be quite serious. For instance, when Martha and Stewart combined their two families, Martha and her children moved into Stewart's home. They considered themselves blessed to have a house large enough to accommodate their stepfamily. Martha rejoiced at the prospect of moving out of her cramped home into her new "love nest." Martha soon discovered that her love nest was turning into a house of horrors:

> "I couldn't just go in and start changing the furniture around. I knew that would have distressed my stepchildren. For their sake, I moved only a few of my own and my children's belongings into the house. At first, I thought it was a perfect place, even though it didn't yet have my touch.
>
> "But things went downhill rapidly. It made me uncomfortable to know that I was sleeping in the same bed in which

Stewart had slept with his ex-wife. I could feel the resentment in my stepchildren when I replaced a picture on the dining-room wall with one that I preferred. It turned out to be a favorite picture of their mother's. More and more, Stewart's ex became an overwhelming presence in the house. It was still her house. It wasn't mine.

"Stewart and I talked about it. He pointed out how ideal the house was, and urged me to stick with it. He said it was just that the place was unfamiliar and that I could redecorate it any way I wanted. Well, one evening at dinner I started telling them all the ideas I had for redecoration and some renovations. They were pretty extensive. My stepchildren exploded with anger. And I knew then it would never work for us to stay in that house.

"Stewart resisted, until I actually threatened to move out and separate for a time until we could sort it all out. When I said that, I think he realized for the first time just how stressed I was. So we moved. My stepchildren were not nearly as bothered by moving to a new house as they had been about redecorating the old one. My only regret is that we didn't get a house big enough so that our two youngest boys could have separate rooms. At least, we saved our marriage. I'm sure it would not have survived if we had stayed in Stewart's house."

Martha and Stewart's move may seem drastic. But let's put it into a different perspective. What was the cost of moving compared to the cost of their marriage breaking up? Your marriage is your calling. You need to do what is necessary to preserve and enrich it.

5) *Stay regularly connected with your spouse.* If you nurture your friendship, you will do this quite naturally. Staying connected, however, goes beyond simple friendship. It means talking together, doing things together, expressing affection, maintaining your sexual relationship, and generally feeling that you are living and working as a team—one flesh, in biblical terms—rather than as two individuals who sometimes cross paths in the effort to maintain a stepfamily.

Here are some examples of how to stay connected from those who have built strong marriages in the context of a stepfamily:

"We have never neglected our marriage for the kids' sake. We have always known that we could only deal well with them if we were on solid ground with our own relationship. One of our rituals is to have dinner together on Friday evening and breakfast together on Saturday morning without the children. Usually, we always eat together as a family at breakfast and dinner, but on those days we all enjoy a break from the routine. And it's a great way for my husband and me to have marriage time.

"I think it also helped our kids to realize that we are truly a couple. That they can't come to one of us and expect sympathy because the other one told them to do something they didn't want to do.

"They're like all children in stepfamilies. Some of them weren't too happy with our marriage. But we've made sure they know we are committed to each other, that this marriage is going to last, and that they're going to love it as much as we do if they work with us" (stepmother of four and mother of five).

"We talk a lot together. We make time for each other. We do volunteer work together at our church. She is truly my best friend, and I believe that I am hers. So we try to do as much together as possible. We never do anything separately if we can do it together" (stepfather of two and father of one).

"We have always taken as much time as possible for ourselves. I think we both learned from our first marriages how fragile a relationship can be if you don't keep working on it. Whenever we have a chance, we go somewhere together—just the two of us. Neither of us ever makes a decision about a commitment of time to something without talking it over first with the other. We have a strong bond, but we never take it for granted" (stepmother of one and mother of three).

"I don't have any children of my own, but I'm a stepfather to my wife's three children, and we have a great relationship. My wife and I have a certain amount of time alone because my stepchildren are off with their father every other weekend; and they spend a certain number of holidays with him. We really enjoy our time alone on the weekends. The holidays are tough sometimes, though, especially when it's their turn to be with their father on Christmas or Thanksgiving.

"But we've found a way to deal with it. We use those times to celebrate our marriage. We take a trip to a warm climate somewhere. We don't let ourselves grieve about not being with the children. We are grateful they are with their father, enjoying themselves. So we focus on having fun together. It's like we have our own private marriage enrichment times" (stepfather of three).

6) Practice forgiveness. As we noted in chapter 7, forgiving your ex is important for your emotional and spiritual well-being. Forgiving your spouse is equally important. Even after Stewart agreed to consider a move to a different house, he dragged his feet in looking for one. He admits now that he kept hoping Martha's feelings would change. It was only after she threatened to leave that he acted. The incident could have been fatal to their marriage if Martha had not been willing to forgive his foot dragging. After all, it had greatly increased her stress. But Martha has a healthy attitude about such things:

> "We both know there will be times when we will disappoint and frustrate each other. You can't have a faultless marriage. We also know that those times when one of us fails the other are not the end of the marriage. You can always recover from them if you keep working together. You also need to forgive each other. It's easier to forgive if you keep in mind that neither one of you is perfect. I think that's what forgiveness is. It's a way of saying, 'Hey, we're both human. So we both need to forgive and we both need to be forgiven.'"

7) Think romance. Both words are important. "Think" is important because you can get so caught up in the demands of stepfamily life that any thoughts of romance are put on hold until an uncertain future date. It isn't that you don't want to be romantic. It isn't that you don't need to be romantic. It's simply that you are pushed in too many directions to indulge in the luxury of romance.

But you're not. If you're too busy or too harried for romance, then you're busier and more harried than you need to be or than you should be. Do whatever it takes to change your life so you have time for romantic experiences.

In most cases, however, we find that romance is neglected because the couple overlooks it in the course of dealing with their other demands and responsibilities. Note the word "other." We regard romance as much a responsibility as anything else because it's a crucial factor in nurturing your marriage.

So think romance. That is, find a way to remind yourself to do something romantic for or with your spouse. A friend, who owns his own business, told us that he knows the importance of expressing appreciation and admiration for his subordinates. But his work demands are so great that he doesn't typically think of doing them. So he found a way to remind himself. In his desk drawer, he placed a memo to himself, containing the phrase, "Give strokes." Every day when he begins work, the memo reminds him of this important task. Similarly, you could write yourself a memo, "Think romance." Or you could use a picture of your spouse to jar your memory. The key is to find some way to remind yourself regularly to think romance.

What, exactly, do you think of when you think romance? A week in Paris? A vacation at the beach? Flowers and dinner out? A surprise gift? No doubt all such things are romantic. But romance isn't limited to things that are time-consuming and expensive. A woman told us that the most romantic thing her husband ever did for her was to send her an unexpected love letter. They have had many romantic experiences, but she cherishes this one above them all. And it only cost him ten minutes of time and the price of a stamp.

The following are among the less expensive and time-consuming experiences that couples in stepfamilies find romantic:

- a quiet evening alone, talking together over a leisurely dinner

- a love note

- an unexpected gift of flowers

- daily prayer together

- going to the movies

- giving each other a massage

- taking a walk and sharing the events of the day

- a special gift

- sitting together and talking in the hot tub at night under the stars

- attending a marriage enrichment weekend together

Obviously, many different kinds of activities contribute to romantic feelings in marriages. From time to time, we hear couples lament, or joke about, the death of romance after years of marriage. We firmly believe that neither the laments nor the jokes reflect reality. The nature of your relationship will naturally change over the years. But romance need never die. In strong marriages, in fact, it doesn't die because the couple won't let it die. They continue to use romance as one of the tools to nurture their marriage. And they use their stable, satisfying marriage as a foundation for building a healthy stepfamily.

In Celebration

The Rewards of Stepfamily Life

I n the course of our research with stepfamilies, we heard a great many horror stories. We have shared some of them with you in this book. However, we also heard about the rewards of stepfamily life. We would like to close with a brief celebration of the stepfamily by sharing with you a few statements from stepparents and stepchildren about the rewards of stepfamily life:

> "I got an instant family when I married Bert, and became the stepmother of his two adolescent children. We've had our struggles, but I am grateful for my family. And I give a lot of the credit for that to Bert, because he always made sure I knew I was as important to him as his children. It's been a wonderful experience."

> "I never wanted a stepmother. I never called my stepmother by any other name than her own—Millie. But we have had a rich experience together. Millie has been, above all things, my dear friend. She taught me to respect myself and to like myself when I was an adolescent and thought I was ugly. I will be forever grateful that Millie has been a part of my life."

> "I was uncertain about marrying a woman with three children. But I loved her deeply, so I decided to take the chance. We talked a lot before we were married about how I would function as a

stepfather. That was twenty years ago. My stepchildren are all young adults. I cherish the years they were at home, and I love them now as if they were my own."

"I was in my teens when my mother married my stepfather. From the beginning, he was like a father to me. He was one of the most wonderful men I have ever known. I could talk to him about anything. He loved me, and I loved him. Now that he is gone, I feel like an important part of my life has been taken away from me."

"We have really done an amazing thing in raising five kids who are close and really like—no, love—each other. Our kids have always gotten along wonderfully. That is the jewel in our crown. We've made our mistakes. But we are thankful to God that our stepfamily is truly a family."

"One of the most joyous experiences of my life was marrying Nan. I had been married before, but I didn't have any children. I gained a daughter when I married Nan. Now I have two grand-children and nineteen years of happiness as a result."

"We had five children between the two of us, and they all really liked each other from the start. We don't think of ourselves as a stepfamily. We're a family. We act like a family. People who meet us don't have a clue that the children don't all belong to both of us unless we tell them. We just get along beautifully."

"My husband and I both brought children to our marriage. When I got pregnant, we thought we were about to add still another child to the group. Then we learned that the son I was carrying would be born with defects and would probably not live long. It was a crisis for all of us. How would we cope? A wonder-ful thing happened. All of the children became more thoughtful, more kind, more caring. One of our son's lasting legacies is that his short life brought us all together in a new way."

Appendix

SUGGESTIONS FOR GROUP DISCUSSION

Chapter 1—"We're Going to Get It Right This Time"

Have each member of the group share what their expectations and hopes for stepfamily life were before their remarriage. Discuss:

1. How realistic were your expectations?

2. Did they change once you were married?

3. What problems have you encountered in your attempt to build a successful stepfamily?

4. Which problems have caused you the greatest difficulties?

5. Are there some things that have generally been problems for most of the group?

Chapter 2—A Tough Way to Begin: The Challenge of Loss

Discuss as a group:

1. As a spouse, what feelings of loss did you experience when you divorced?

2. Did you work through these feelings before you remarried?

3. If you are the custodial parent, did remarriage add to your sense of loss in any way? How have you handled these feelings?

5. Have you experienced any sense of loss since you remarried and assumed the responsibilities of being a stepparent? How have you dealt with your feelings?

6. What feelings of loss do you think your children experienced when you divorced? When you remarried?

7. What did you do to help them cope with their feelings of loss? Have your efforts been successful?

8. Have any of the feelings of loss that resulted from your divorce or remarriage affected your stepfamily relationship? How?

9. Have the group role play a "family meeting." Assign family member parts to volunteers in the group, allow each to talk about their sense of loss, and then share any benefits they gained from this exercise.

Chapter 3—Not an Ordinary Family: The Challenge of Adjustment

As a group, discuss:

1. Did you have any fantasies about stepfamily life before your remarriage? What were they?

2. Do you think any of these fantasies have caused difficulties for your marriage or for your stepfamily life? In what ways?

3. Is it hard for you to accept that your stepfamily will always be "different" from a biological family? Why?

4. Have you struggled to love your stepchildren or to have them love you? Have your struggles been successful? Why or why not?

5. How has agape love helped you function as a stepparent?

6. As a stepparent, what kind of situations stretch your patience to the breaking point? How do you deal with these situations?

7. Respond to this statement: "Expect to be a stepparent—not a parent nor a super-parent." Why is it important to remember the difference?

8. Have you found creative ways to handle conflict in your stepfamily?

9. What have been your greatest rewards as a member of a stepfamily?

Chapter 4—Who Am I?: The Challenge of Personal Identity
Divide the group into males and females and have each discuss the following:

1. How did the breakup of your first marriage affect your sense of personal identity?

2. How did remarriage affect your sense of personal identity?

3. Compare your experience of being a spouse in a stepfamily with the experience in your first marriage? Has this experience affected your sense of identity?

4. How has becoming a stepparent affected your sense of personal identity?

5. In what ways do you think being part of a stepfamily has affected your children's sense of identity?

Provide sufficient time for the men's and women's groups to discuss these questions, but allow approximately thirty minutes for the group to reconvene and discuss their findings. Did the experiences of men and women differ in any or all of these categories? How? Why do you think this is the case?

Chapter 5— Who Are We?: The Challenge of Family Identity
At the beginning of this group session, work as couples. Let each couple chart their stepfamily relationships and then discuss the following:

1. With which family members are we in frequent contact?

2. How many members do we see only infrequently or never?

3. How do you account for the differences in the frequency of contact that you have with your various family members?

4. What do you see as the core of your family identity?

After the couples have sufficient time to do this exercise, have the group reconvene and share their findings. If time permits, discuss as a group:

1. How you have handled the question of what your stepchildren should call you?

2. The techniques you have used to create a sense of identity in your stepfamily;

3. What problems you have encountered in establishing a sense of stepfamily identity.

Chapter 6—"If I Love You, Do I Stop Loving Him?": The Challenge of Loyalty Conflicts

As a group, discuss the following:

1. Do you think your children have experienced any loyalty conflicts since they became part of a stepfamily? If so, what kinds?

2. How have you dealt with your children's loyalty conflicts within the context of your stepfamily?

3. If your children haven't experienced any loyalty conflicts since they became a part of a stepfamily, how do you account for this?

4. Have you, as a stepparent, experienced any loyalty conflicts since you became a part of a stepfamily? How have you handled these?

5. Have you, as a spouse, experienced any loyalty conflicts since you became a part of a stepfamily? If so, how have you dealt with these?

6. The authors suggest that you should be proactive in helping family members confront and deal with their loyalty conflicts. Share with the group any proactive measures you have taken with stepfamily members or with extend family to deal with this problem.

Chapter 7—The Ex Factor: The Challenge of Former Spouses

Divide the group into males and females and have each group discuss the following questions:

1. Is your spouse in any way still tied to his or her ex-spouse? In what ways?

2. Is this a problem for you? In what ways?

3. How do you deal with this problem?

Provide sufficient time to discuss these questions, but allow approximately forty-five minutes for the group to reconvene and discuss:

1. Do men and women differ in the ways they experience their ex spouse? If so, in what ways? Why do you think this is the case?

2. Are there differences in the way males and females deal with problems associated with a distressing ex-spouse?

3. The authors suggest that, in dealing with your ex-spouse, it is important to forgive him or her for past ill-treatment. Has such forgiveness been difficult for you? Why or why not? What help can you offer to others who are having a difficult time forgiving their ex-spouses?

Chapter 8—Can We Make It?: The Challenge of Resources

At the beginning of the session, have each couple work alone on a personal inventory of their resources by discussing the following:

1. Time. Do we spend enough time together as a stepfamily? What can we change in order to increase the quantity and quality of the time we have together?

2. Money. Do we manage our money well? Are there extra burdens on our income because we are a stepfamily? What can we do to improve the economic relations in our home?

3. Social Network. Do we have a strong supportive network of family and friends? If not, what can we do to change the situation?

4. Spiritual Resources. Do we, as a stepfamily, worship, pray, and study the Bible together? Do we openly discuss together our spiritual concerns as well as our spiritual joys? How can we increase and make greater use of our spiritual resources?

Provide sufficient time for each couple to discuss these questions. Then reconvene the group to share and discuss each couple's resource inventory. Have someone write down the group's judgment of the best suggestions in each of the four areas and provide each couple with a copy of the list.

Chapter 9—"You're Not My Father": The Challenge of Stepparenting

As a group, discuss the following:

1. What expectations did you have when you became a stepparent?

2. Were these expectations realistic? Why or why not?

3. What are the biggest challenges you have faced as a stepparent?

4. How have you dealt with them?

5. How is discipline handled in your stepfamily?

6. Has your arrangement worked well? Why or why not?

7. Can you make this statement: "I feel that my stepchild and I are friends?" If so, how did you make it happen?

8. Do you ever use humor in dealing with the challenges of being a stepparent? If the answer is yes, share some examples with the group.

Chapter 10: Becoming One Flesh in the Midst of Turmoil: The Challenge of Marital Intimacy
As a couple, complete the following marital inventory:

1. Are we each other's best friend?
2. Are we each committed to the institution of marriage?
3. Are we each committed to the well-being of the other?
4. Are we each meeting the other's need for affection and sex?
5. Are we each satisfied with the quality of our communication together?

Then, talk together about ways you can improve in one or more of the areas.

Reconvene as a group, and have those couples who are willing share the results of their discussion. If time allows, discuss the following:

1. What strains has being a stepfamily put on your marital relationship?
2. In the midst of the many challenges, what ways have you found to nurture your marriage?

Additional Resources

Make use of the following resources for strengthening your own stepfamily and also for stepfamily support-group discussions.

ORGANIZATION
The Stepfamily Association of America, 650 J Street, Suite 205, Lincoln, NE 68508

For a small fee, you can join this organization, receive their quarterly publication *Stepfamilies*, and order other resources they offer.

BOOKS
Beer, William R. *Strangers In the House: The World of Stepsiblings and Half-Siblings.* New Brunswick, N.J.: Transaction Publishers, 1989.

Dunn, Dick. *Willing To Try Again.* Valley Forge, Pa.: Judson Press, 1993.

Engel, Margorie. *Weddings A Family Affair: The New Etiquette for Second Marriages and Couples with Divorced Parents.* North Hollywood, Calif.: Wilshire Publications, 1998.

Estess, Patricia Schiff. *Money Advice for Your Successful Remarriage.* Cincinnati, Ohio: Betterway Books, 1996.

Larson, Jeffry H., James O. Anderson and Ann Morgan. *Effective Stepparenting.* New York: Family Service America, 1984.

Mulford, Philippa Greene. *Keys to Successful Stepmothering.* Hauppauge, N.Y.: Barron's Educational Series, 1996.

Prickhard, Carl E. *Keys to Successful Stepfathering.* Hauppauge, N.Y.: Barron's Educational Series, 1997.

MEDIA

An American Stepfamily. Video. Films for the Humanities & Sciences.

Engels, Margorie. *Steps Ahead with Daisy Petals: They Love Me—College Expenses; They Love Me Not.* Inheritance. Audio tapes. Stepfamily Association of America.

Positive Steps: Solutions To Establishing Positive Stepfamilies. An Internet resource focusing on stepparent research and support at <http://www.positivestep.com>.

LIBRARIES

Check your local public and college libraries for materials. There are many good articles in popular publications. Look for them in *The Reader's Guide to Periodical Literature.* Libraries may also have books and audio-visual materials of various kinds.